IMAGE TRANSFER WORKSHOP

DARLENE OLIVIA McELROY

AND

SANDRA DURAN WILSON

NORTH LIGHT BOOKS

Cincinnati, Ohio

www.mycraftivity.com

13 12 11 10 09   5 4 3

Distributed in Canada by Fraser Direct
100 Armstrong Avenue
Georgetown, ON, Canada L7G 5S4
Tel: (905) 877-4411

Distributed in the U.K. and Europe by David & Charles
Brunel House, Newton Abbot, Devon, TQ12 4PU, England
Tel: (+44) 1626 323200, Fax: (+44) 1626 323319
E-mail: postmaster@davidandcharles.co.uk

Distributed in Australia by Capricorn Link
P.O. Box 704, S. Windsor, NSW 2756 Australia
Tel: (02) 4577-3555

METRIC CONVERSION

TO CONVERT	TO	MULTIPLY BY
Inches	Centimeters	2.54
Centimeters	Inches	0.4
Feet	Centimeters	30.5
Centimeters	Feet	0.03
Yards	Meters	0.9
Meters	Yards	1.1
Sq. Inches	Sq. Centimeters	6.45
Sq. Centimeters	Sq. Inches	0.16
Sq. Feet	Sq. Meters	0.09
Sq. Meters	Sq. Feet	10.8
Sq. Yards	Sq. Meters	0.8
Sq. Meters	Sq. Yards	1.2
Pounds	Kilograms	0.45
Kilograms	Pounds	2.2
Ounces	Grams	28.3
Grams	Ounces	0.035

Library of Congress Cataloging-in-Publication Data
McElroy, Darlene Olivia.
  Image transfer workshop / Darlene Olivia McElroy and Sandra Duran Wilson. -- 1st ed.
      p. cm.
  Includes index.
  ISBN 978-1-60061-160-5 (pbk. : alk. paper)
  1. Handicraft. 2. Transfer-printing. I. Duran Wilson, Sandra. II. Title.
  TT880.M156 2009
  745.5--dc22
                  2009003331

Editor: Julie Hollyday
Designer: Marissa Bowers
Production Coordinator: Greg Nock
Photographer: Christine Polomsky, Ric Deliatoni
Photo Stylist: Jan Nickum

fw
media
www.fwmedia.com

DEDICATIONS

FROM DARLENE OLIVIA McELROY:

To my sister-mom, Lou Taylor, who always believed in me and taught me to dream in color. To the love of my life, Dave Stearns, for his undying support and encouragement. To Marina Farr, my niece and the next generation of artists—go for it, girl.

FROM SANDRA DURAN WILSON:

To my incredible husband, Mark—you are my greatest inspiration in life and your encouragement, love and support fill my life with color. To my family, who always believed in my artistic path.

ACKNOWLEDGMENTS

Thank you to Bonnie Teitelbaum, our greatest assistant and asset; you kept us on track and provided another perspective. We couldn't have done it without you and the incredible F+W team. We would like to thank Tonia Davenport for getting us on board; Julie Hollyday, our editor extraordinaire; Christine Polomsky, our photographer, who kept us going and laughing; and thanks to all of our students, who gave us inspiration to create this book.

ABOUT THE AUTHORS

DARLENE OLIVIA McELROY, comes from an old New Mexico family of storytellers and artists. She began making art the first time she found a wall and a drawing instrument. Her grandfather, a painter on Catalina Island, was her mentor and taught her to play and experiment with art.

Darlene attended the Art Center College of Design in Pasadena, then worked as an illustrator both in the U.S. and in Paris. The influence of her background and her travels is evident in her art.

She lives and works in Santa Fe and creates new life stories with her husband Dave, her three dogs, Oso, Taco and Bernie, and two birds.

SANDRA DURAN WILSON has been painting since she was very young, when she went on location with her great-aunt, the Texas landscape artist Santa Duran, to paint the Spanish missions and landscapes around San Antonio where she grew up. Sandra came from a family of artists and scientists, so both views of the world influence her. She often looked through her father's microscope and painted what she saw.

She holds degrees in both science and fine art, which provides the foundations of her explorations and experiments in art.

Sandra's home and studio are in Santa Fe, where she shares her adventures with her husband Mark and their feline friends Muki and Niki.

CONTENTS

INTRODUCTION

Writing this book has been a fun-filled adventure for us exploring familiar techniques and discovering new ones in the process. We played, laughed, wondered why, scratched our heads and howled at some of our bloopers. We complied 35 techniques to transfer images.

Transfers can add another layer of texture, imagery and mystery to your composition. They are great ways to use family photographs, create original journal or book pages, enhance artwork and even create jewelry. As artists we have very different styles, so we wanted to illustrate how the same methods could accommodate those diverse styles. Artists of all mediums, from journals and scrapbooks to quilting, jewelry, sculpture and painting, will find inspiration in art born from transfers.

We explore transfer techniques that use materials that you may have on hand, such as freezer paper and plastic wrap, as well as options that use copy machines and printmaking methods. Some of the techniques, like gel and gesso transfers, have been around for a long time and are still proven methods to get a consistent result. Some of the techniques that worked in the past, like water and ink-jet photo transfers, do not work well now due to changes in technology. We have found alternative methods and have even come up with some new variations on transfers. Some techniques render similar results, leaving you to wonder, "Why would I use this method instead of that one?" The answer may depend on the supplies you have on hand or a personal preference. We evaluate when a method isn't working and provide tips for altering and enhancing your transfers.

There are basic ways to create transfers: glues and mediums, heat, solvents, and assorted methods from stenciling to rusting. When you can use all the different methods, you can choose which method will best meet your needs. It is like having a brand new toolbox filled with everything you want. You might use a single technique or combine several to get your desired results. Knowledge is your best asset: Understanding why some things work or don't work can lead you to break the rules and make new discoveries. Our greatest hope is that you explore and accept all those possibilities—including the happy accidents. We encourage you to play, create and let us know what you discover. Visit us at imagetransferworkshop.com.

HOW THIS BOOK IS SET UP

Each technique has its own special qualities. We'd like to show you how the book is set up so you'll know what to look for where, when and why.

PROJECT INTRODUCTION: WHAT IS THIS TECHNIQUE ALL ABOUT?

This brief introduction explains the technique and the type of image it may produce. Be sure to check here to find out what kind of printer or copier works best with the transfer technique, as the wrong type may result in a poor transfer or no transfer at all.

LIMITATIONS: WHAT ARE POTENTIAL ISSUES WITH THIS TECHNIQUE?

Transfers can cast a whole range of finished images, from limited sizes to dreamy lines. Look here to see if the technique will reproduce the image to your liking.

SURFACE OPTIONS: WHAT SURFACE WILL THE TECHNIQUE WORK ON?

Surfaces can be as sturdy as rock or as delicate as rice paper. Check here for recommendations on what surfaces the technique will work best. Transfer surfaces may include canvas, Plexiglas, smooth metal, plastic wrap, tin foil, and papers, including gampi/silk tissue, printmaking and watercolor papers, and rice paper.

ARCHIVAL QUALITY: WILL THIS TRANSFER STAND THE TEST OF TIME?

Most artists want to know: Will this image last? Does the image transfer fade easily, or will it deteriorate over a longer period of time? Exposure to UV light, moisture and acidity of papers, or pH, will affect pigments over time. Some pigments are more lightfast than others meaning they won't fade from print. The archival quality of each transfer is broken down into three categories:

Low archival quality. Images are more prone to fading over time. This happens in ink-jet prints that are not printed on adequately primed surfaces and are not protected by a varnish or proper framing. This is not a scientific estimate, but images with a low archival rating may fade within a few years without protection. You can always enhance the archival durability with preservative sprays and varnishes.

TROUBLESHOOTING

WHAT HAPPENED TO YOUR TRANSFER? WE'LL TELL YOU!

One of the best features of this book is the troubleshooting sections. In these sections, you'll find tips and tricks to save transfers-gone-wrong. In the event you'll have to start a transfer over, we'll tell you what to look out for next time to achieve great transfers!

Medium archival quality. Uses more lightfast inks, proper preparation with sprays and care in mounting and/or framing. Most magazine images and toner color copies fall into this category. You should have no problems for decades.

High archival quality. Uses lightfast paints and carbon or black toner prints. These should last seventy-five years or more.

Using Krylon Preserve It! on ink-jet prints, magazines and found papers increases the lightfastness, and Krylon Make It Acid-Free! helps preserve papers by neutralizing the pH. If you are making a card or page in a book that will not be exposed to UV light, don't worry about the archival quality, but if you are using any of these techniques for finished art for sale, use the preservatives and a UV-resistant varnish. We like Golden Archival Spray Varnish; it comes in matte, satin or gloss sheens. Several coats are best.

8

NOTES: WHAT OTHER INFORMATION SHOULD I CONSIDER?

Here you'll find important information that will help you as you complete each technique. Useful notes may include information on timing, reminders to flip images (especially if they have words and numbers) and other tips for completing a successful transfer.

MATERIALS: WHAT DO I NEED TO COMPLETE THIS TRANSFER TECHNIQUE?

Materials and tools for image transfer techniques are as varied as the techniques themselves. From the uncommon uses for household items to the mundane art items rehashed. Be sure to read the materials list carefully, and gather all the materials before you begin each technique.

common tools and materials

While the techniques in this book use a variety of materials to make fabulous image transfers, we make good use of some basic tools and materials in most of the processes. If you have the following items, you're in a good place to start:

Materials:

soft gel (gloss)

polymer medium (gloss)

workable fixative

UV-resistant varnish or spray

Tools:

lots of copy paper

brayer, bone folder or large spoon

spray bottle with water

paintbrush

palette knife

fine grit sandpaper

scissors

paper towels

iron

a note about printers and copiers

When working with image transfers, it is important to know which type of printed image you can use for the various techniques. To know this, you must know what kind of printers you will have access to—either an ink-jet printer or copier or a laser printer or copier. Throughout the book, we'll let you know which printer or copier will work for the techniques; in some techniques, only one will work; for other techniques, both may work.

Images produced by ink-jet copiers and printers are water soluble. You must spray ink-jet images with a workable fixative if you don't want them to smear. Laser images are created with heat and dry toner. You can put water on them, and they will not smear.

When working with printers and copiers, you will find that they are all different. If you are trying a technique and it is not working, try a different machine. Don't make a lot of copies until you find a machine that works for you. Sometimes, increasing the toner level or using a color copier, even to print black-and-white images, will help the transfer.

GLUES AND MEDIUMS

Glues, tapes and mediums are used to in image transfers to hold the ink from copies or magazines while allowing the paper to be eliminated. This is a simple method to build history into your project; it can create transparent or opaque layers that can be used in many different mediums from painting to journal pages.

Some of these techniques are prized for their clarity and ease of use, such as *Clear Contact Paper* or *Clear Packing Tape* (page 12), while others can be used to create architectural features, like *Gel Skin* (page 20). We use *Dry Gel, Gesso and Caulk* (page 17) and *Paint* (page 24) transfers the most—Sandra finds gesso transfers to be a great way to begin a project. We love to sand, scrape and burn edges and surfaces to create more drama and mystery. *Transparency With Gel* (page 26) transfers are fun, fast and great in journals. Remember that the ink-jet copies release with water, and the toner-based images need to be dried.

Many of the mediums used in this section are also used to bond other transfer techniques to backgrounds. We commonly use soft gel (gloss) and liquid polymer medium to adhere images. Consider buying some containers of each to have on hand. We use gloss gels and mediums because, when dry, they are the most clear. Matte or satin mediums may be used, but realize that the imagery will be diffused. Be sure to check materials lists to get the right adhesive for each transfer throughout the book.

CLEAR CONTACT PAPER OR CLEAR PACKING TAPE

These are two of the easiest transfer techniques, and they use products we often have available at home. You can use either toner-based or magazine images (with the exception of magazine images that are coated with either a varnish or plastic coating).

Packing tape is thinner and more transparent than the contact paper, but it has restricted width.

After applying the packing tape or contact paper to the image face, the trick is to burnish the image well so the ink sticks to the adhesive. You can actually see this happen.

MAGIC TIME | *Clear packing tape transfer, stamps and Lazertran transfer.*
ARTWORK BY DARLENE OLIVIA McELROY

LIMITATIONS
Clear packing tape is limited to the width of the tape, though you can add rows of additional tape to make it wider. Clear contact paper can leave a slightly fuzzy image. Both leave an edge on the finished piece, but this can be minimized with additional layers and finish.

SURFACE OPTIONS
This transfer technique works on any surface.

ARCHIVAL QUALITY
For clear packing tape, the quality is low to medium. Coat images with UV-resistant spray before putting the tape on the image to help the quality.

With clear contact paper, carbon black-and-white copies are lightfast. Magazine images and color copies can be sprayed with a UV-resistant spray prior to transferring to improve lightfastness.

NOTES
For a distressed look, sand the image transferred to the contact paper or packing tape.

Don't dump paper rubbings into the sink.

Different brands of contact paper work differently, some better than others. Don't use contact paper that can be repositioned. Try out a few brands that are meant to be permanent.

Materials ✳ toner-based or magazine image ✳ clear contact paper or clear packing tape ✳ background surface ✳ bone folder or large spoon ✳ sandpaper ✳ spray bottle of water ✳ soft cloth (optional) ✳ soft gel (gloss) or polymer medium (gloss) ✳ paintbrush ✳ scissors

2 / BURNISH IMAGE

Using a bone folder or a large spoon, burnish the image thoroughly. You want the ink from the image to transfer completely to the contact paper or packing tape.

1 / PREPARE IMAGE

Select the image to be transferred.

IF USING CONTACT PAPER: Use scissors to cut the contact paper to the size needed. Peel off the backing and put sticky side down on the face of the image.

IF USING PACKING TAPE: Layer the packing tape to the size needed to cover the image.

3 / SAND IMAGE BACKING

Using the sandpaper, lightly rough up the back of the image to break up the paper backing.

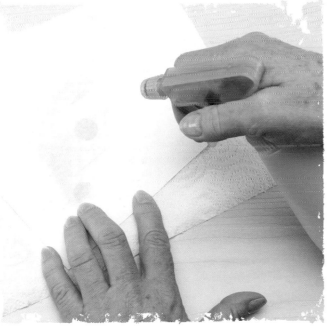

4 / MOISTEN PAPER BACKING

Using the spray bottle with water, moisten the paper backing.

5 / REMOVE PAPER

Using your fingers or a soft cloth, rub off the wet paper, leaving the ink on the contact paper.

13

6 / APPLY MEDIUM TO SURFACE

Using a paintbrush, apply polymer medium or soft gel onto the background surface.

7 / APPLY IMAGE TO SURFACE

Lay the contact paper or packing tape image sticky-side down. Using a paintbrush, smooth out the image to the surface with polymer medium or soft gel.

TROUBLESHOOTING

MISSING PIECES OF THE IMAGE?

If you're missing pieces of the image after removing the paper, there are two possible explanations: Either you didn't burnish the image enough, or you rubbed too hard while removing the paper backing. This result can actually add more texture and interest to your transfer, but if you're looking for a near-perfect transfer follow this advice: Burnish hard and several times in step 2. Be gentle when removing the paper in step 5—take off one layer of paper, then let it dry. Repeat steps 4 and 5 until all the paper is removed.

GHOST IMAGES

If you don't remove all of the paper, you'll have a ghost-like paper residue. Let the paper backing dry, then repeat steps 4 and 5.

OTHER TIPS

Some copy machines and printers use less toner and may not work as well for this technique. If you're having problems with the transfer, try a different printer, or try a print shop: Ask them to increase the toner or use a different type of paper.

If you want to paint over areas of the transfer, roughen the surface slightly with fine sandpaper so the tape or contact paper can hold the paint. You could also paint a layer of clear gesso on top and let it dry, with or without sanding it first.

14

DIRECT GEL, GESSO AND CAULK

This technique works with ink-jet images. With soft gel or clear caulk the background will show through. With gesso or white caulk the background will be white or whatever color you tint the medium.

Timing and weather are big variables in this transfer. Because of changes in the season or climate, you will find that you might have to adjust your timing.

LIMITATIONS
This technique does not make a perfect transfer.

SURFACE OPTIONS
You can do a direct transfer to about any surface that you can apply the mediums to, such as canvas, paper, wood, Plexiglas or sanded metal.

ARCHIVAL QUALITY
Low quality but can be enhanced with a UV-resistant spray.

NOTES
Remember that the background will show through the light areas of the image.

The image will be reproduced backwards, but you can flip the image when making copies.

Because of changing technology you might have problems with some printer paper, especially new glossy ones. Printing the image onto plain copy paper yields the best results.

SONG AND DANCE | *Direct gel transfers, collage and embellishments*
ARTWORK BY SANDRA DURAN WILSON

Materials ❋ ink-jet image ❋ background surface ❋ soft gel (gloss), gesso or clear caulk ❋ paintbrush ❋ brayer ❋ scissors

2 / APPLY MEDIUM TO BACKGROUND

Using a paintbrush, apply a medium layer of gesso, gel medium or clear caulk onto the background surface. If the layer is too thin, the medium will dry too fast; if it's too thick, the medium will ooze out when burnishing.

1 / SELECT IMAGE

Choose a color or black-and-white image from an ink-jet printer. Using the scissors, cut out the desired image. You may leave a border around the image for easy handling.

3 / APPLY IMAGE

Immediately lay the image ink-side down onto the gesso/gel/caulk.

TROUBLESHOOTING

MISSING PARTS OF THE IMAGE?

If you leave the paper on too long, it will stick to the medium. If that happens, you might be able to peel off a layer of the paper. Then you have a transfer with a thin layer of paper on top. You can let this dry, then put a layer of polymer medium gloss on top to make it more transparent.

These transfers are trickier now because new technology makes the printing inks stick to the paper better.

4 / BURNISH IMAGE

Using the brayer, rub down the image for approximately 30 seconds to 1 minute. Start with a light touch, and check to see how it is transferring. Apply more pressure if needed.

5 / CHECK TRANSFER

Hold the edge of the paper and peel back a corner to reveal the image transfer. Burnish for an additional 30 seconds if necessary.

DRY GEL, GESSO AND CAULK

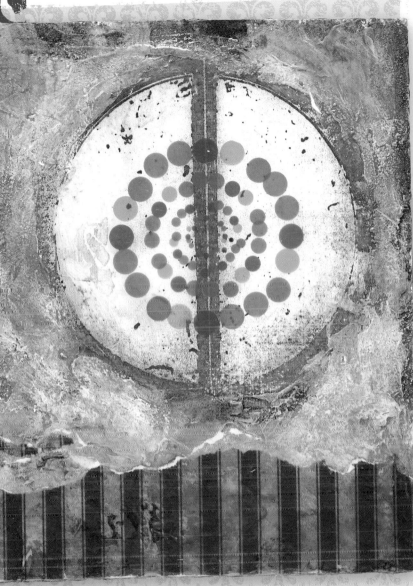

THE BEGINNING | *Dry gesso transfer, dry gel transfer on molding paste background*

ARTWORK BY SANDRA DURAN WILSON

The important thing to remember with this technique is whether you want the toner-based or magazine transfer to be opaque or transparent. Gel or clear caulk creates a transparent transfer and you will be able to see what is underneath it in the lighter areas of the transfer. With gesso or white caulk, which you can tint, you will not be able to see anything underneath because the mediums are opaque.

LIMITATIONS

It's important for the image to be burnished down well and for the medium to be thoroughly dry before removing the paper backing.

This technique doesn't work on magazine images that have a varnish or plastic coating, such as those found on the front and back cover.

SURFACE OPTIONS

This transfer technique works on most surfaces.

ARCHIVAL QUALITY

Medium to high; UV-resistant spray adds to the archival quality.

NOTES

Your chosen image will be reproduced backwards. You can flip it back with computer editing software or a printer.

High-contrast images work well.

Don't dump paper rubbings down the sink drain.

For a wrinkled effect, pat down the image lightly, and don't burnish.

Materials ✳ **toner-based or magazine image** ✳ **background of choice** ✳ **gesso, soft gel (gloss) or caulk** ✳ **paintbrush** ✳ **brayer** ✳ **sandpaper** ✳ **spray bottle of water** ✳ **soft cloth** ✳ **scissors**

1 / PREPARE BACKGROUND

Choose a toner-based or magazine image. Using the scissors, cut the image to the desired shape and size. Using the paintbrush, apply gesso, gel or caulk to the background surface.

2 / APPLY IMAGE TO SURFACE

Lay the paper image-side down onto the prepared surface.

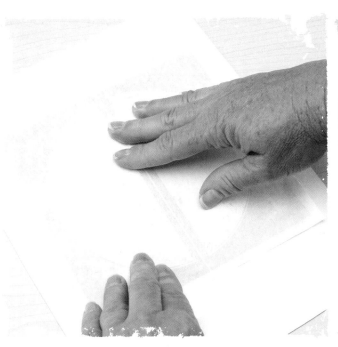

3 / SMOOTH IMAGE

Using your hands, smooth the image down on to the background. If desired, you can use a brayer.

4 / SAND IMAGE BACKING

Let the image thoroughly dry, which could take as long as 24 hours. Using the sandpaper, lightly rough up the back of the image.

5 / MOISTEN IMAGE BACKING

Using the spray bottle with water, moisten the back of the image.

6 / RUB OFF PAPER

Using the soft cloth, gently rub off a layer of paper. Let the image dry. Repeat steps 5 and 6 to rub off any additional paper layers.

TROUBLESHOOTING

WHY WON'T THE IMAGE STAY?

If there is not enough gesso/gel/caulk or if the medium has dried in spots, the image will not transfer. Make sure you have enough medium, and lay the image ink-side down immediately after applying it.

MISTAKES CAN BE MAGIC

Though you will usually want most of the paper backing to be removed, sometimes leaving some on can have a wonderful effect.

If the image wasn't rubbed down well when using magazine images, you will get ripples in your image. When the paper is rubbed off, you will get an abstract appearance.

If this happy mistake doesn't suit your taste, here are two tips to get the wrinkles out: Use the spray bottle to mist the image before placing it facedown onto the surface. If wetting the image is too messy for you, simply try burnishing harder.

TEST

Soft gel (with dry magazine just patted on) and fabric crayon transfers

ARTWORK BY
DARLENE OLIVIA
McELROY AND
SANDRA DURAN WILSON

GEL SKIN

Gel skins can be made using toner-based or magazine images. As we show with this art piece, you can use a black-and-white image, then paint the back of the gel skin to add color and texture to your finished artwork. Try embedding flexible materials in the gel skin before it dries, then you can shape the skin once it has dried completely.

LIMITATIONS
The skin has an edge when pasted down that can be minimized with additional gels and mediums; or, if you prefer, you can play up the edge in the artwork.

SURFACE OPTIONS
The skin can be adhered to almost any surface in addition to being rolled or worked into a sculptural shape.

ARCHIVAL QUALITY
High archival quality if you use a toner-based image, especially a black image.

NOTES
Remember that the background shows through light areas of the image, which will become transparent.

Using soft gel (gloss) will keep your images clear even with two to three layers. You can alter the finish by applying a satin or matte varnish as your final coat.

If copying the image, it will be reproduced backwards. The image can be flipped using the setting on the copy machine.

Don't dump paper rubbings down the sink drain.

COUNTING STONES | *Gel skin, collage and gum bichromate print on handmade paper*
ARTWORK BY SANDRA DURAN WILSON

Materials ✳ **toner-based or magazine image** ✳ **scissors** ✳ **background surface** ✳ **soft gel (gloss)** ✳ **paintbrush** ✳ **sandpaper** ✳ **spray bottle with water**

2 / SAND BACKING

Let the final layer of soft gel dry thoroughly, which could take overnight or longer. Using the sandpaper, gently roughen the back of the image.

1 / PREPARE IMAGE

Choose a toner-based or magazine image. Using scissors, cut the image to the desired size. Using the paintbrush, apply the soft gel to the image. Let the layer dry. Add 2–3 more layers of the soft gel, allowing each layer to dry thoroughly (the gel will become clear when it is completely dry).

3 / MOISTEN IMAGE BACKING

Using a spray bottle with water, moisten the back of the image.

4 / RUB OFF BACKING

Using your fingers, rub off the paper backing.

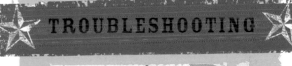

WHAT CAN I DO TO GET ALL OF THE PAPER OFF?

If there is too much paper on the back, let it dry completely, and repeat steps 3 and 4 until all of the paper is removed.

You can also use some clear polymer medium to make the paper backing more transparent. If too much paper is left on, this will not work well.

MY IMAGE IS WRINKLED

To eliminate wrinkles, wet the paper before you place it facedown on the surface.

DIGITAL GROUND

Grounds are coatings that allow you to directly transfer images onto difficult surfaces such as tin foil, paint, gel skin, wood veneer, plastic and other hard-to-transfer-to surfaces using an ink-jet printer. It comes in clear and white. Remember the white covers up anything that is underneath it.

LIMITATIONS
The size of the printer feed and the type of printer feed will affect this technique. It does not work well with a c-curve feed; it works best with a direct feed. The printer can leave "pizza wheel" marks on some substrates.

SURFACE OPTIONS
Works on foil, paint and gel skin, wood veneer, plastic, metallic paper, absorbent ground and painted or collaged surfaces using an ink-jet printer. Be sure to use the appropriate Digital Ground for your chosen surface.

ARCHIVAL QUALITY
Medium archival quality, but a UV-resistant gel or spray will improve the archival quality.

NOTES
If you want to use this technique with tin foil or gel skins (see page 20), place the foil or gel skin to a sheet of copy paper. Using the cellophane tape, secure the edge that will go through the feeder first and tape 2" (5cm) on the sides.

THE GIFT | *Painted and stamped canvas and Golden Digital Ground for Non-Porus Surfaces*

ARTWORK BY DARLENE OLIVIA McELROY

Materials ✳ ink-jet printer ✳ background surface ✳ Golden Digital Ground ✳ paintbrush ✳ workable fixative

TIP
If you can't find Golden Digital Ground, you can also use inkAID for this technique.

1 / APPLY DIGITAL GROUND

Using the paintbrush, apply the Golden Digital Ground to the background surface. Often one coat is sufficient. If a second coat is necessary, let the first coat dry before applying the second.

2 / PRINT IMAGE

Allow the Digital Ground to dry thoroughly. Using an ink-jet printer, print the image onto the background surface. Spray it with the workable fixative. Let the image dry thoroughly. Embellish the image as desired.

TROUBLESHOOTING

I JUST MADE A MESS. WHAT HAPPENED?

If your image smears, there are two possible culprits: Either you didn't add the Digital Ground or you used a toner-based printer.

To fix this, wipe off the ink and repeat steps 1 and 2. Also, make sure you are using an ink-jet printer. A laser printer will only yield the same muddy results.

WHAT ARE THESE SQUIGGLY LINES WHEN I USE TIN FOIL?

If you're using tin foil, you may get "pizza wheel" imprints from your printer. You can take these wheels out, but your warranty is usually rendered invalid if you do.

In general, you should use the manual feed to make sure your transfer surface goes through the printer properly.

TIP

If you're looking for a better archival quality, use a palette knife to apply a thin layer of Golden Gel Topcoat with UVLS. Let it dry thoroughly before embellishing.

PAINT

The difference between a paint transfer and gel/gesso/caulk transfer is that the paint has less body so it requires painting both the image face and the background before laying the image facedown on the background. Kind of like a paint sandwich.

LIMITATIONS

Lighter colors work better than dark because the lighter colors in an image are more transparent. With a dark paint you will lose a lot of the image.

SURFACE OPTIONS

Works well on canvas, panel and Plexiglas.

ARCHIVAL QUALITY

High archival quality, but we always recommend a UV-resistant finish.

NOTES

Image will be reproduced backwards , but it can be flipped when making copies.

Because you must wet the back of the image to remove the paper back, this does not work well on most paper backgrounds with the exception of watercolor or printmaking papers.

Don't dump paper rubbings down the sink drain.

SUMMER AFTERNOON | *Paint transfer, stamping and paint*
ARTWORK BY DARLENE OLIVIA McELROY

Materials ✲ **toner-based or magazine image** ✲ **background surface** ✲ **acrylic paint** ✲ **paintbrush** ✲ **brayer** ✲ **sandpaper** ✲ **spray bottle with water**

TIP

This is a great technique for covering up areas of a project that aren't working. Paint over the area, and apply the transfer. The paint will cover up the background.

1 / PAINT IMAGE AND BACKGROUND

Using a paintbrush and an acrylic paint of your choice, paint both the background surface and the face of the image.

2 / BRAYER IMAGE

Immediately place the image facedown onto the background surface. Using the brayer, smooth the paper onto the surface.

3 / SAND IMAGE BACKING

Allow the image to dry thoroughly, which usually takes several hours. Using the sandpaper, lightly rough up the back of the image.

4 / MOISTEN IMAGE BACKING

Using the spray bottle with water, moisten the back of the paper.

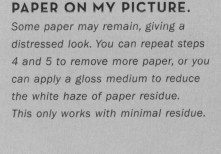

5 / REMOVE PAPER

Using your finger, rub off the paper to reveal the image. The paper will come off in layers. Repeat steps 4 and 5 to remove as much paper as possible.

TRANSPARENCY WITH GEL

This ink-jet transfer technique gives you an abstracted image. Some areas may be very clear and others begin to move and shift. If you are looking for a great way to start a painting or create a layer—and you are open to surprises—then this is a technique for you.

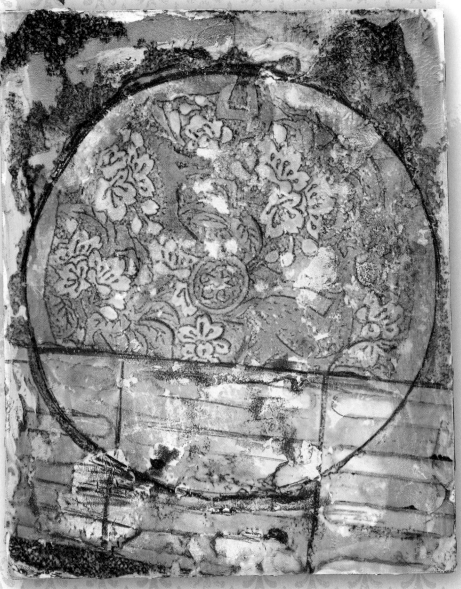

FLOWER WHEEL | *Gel transfer from ink-jet transparency, paint and texture mediums*

ARTWORK BY SANDRA DURAN WILSON

Materials ✳ ink-jet printer ✳ multipurpose transparency film (for all printers) ✳ background surface of choice ✳ soft gel (gloss) ✳ paintbrush ✳ brayer

LIMITATIONS
You are limited to the size of the transparency film and your printer, but you can "tile" the image to make a larger image.

SURFACE OPTIONS
This technique works on water-based paintings, paper, wood, properly prepared metal and Plexiglas.

ARCHIVAL QUALITY
An ink-jet image's quality is low, but you can always increase the archival quality with the application of a UV protective varnish.

NOTES
The success of this transfer depends on the proper thickness of the soft gel in relation to the absorbency of your background. If you are putting this onto paper (high absorbency), you will need a medium layer of soft gel. If you are transferring onto Plexiglas (non-absorbent), you should use a thin layer.

Temperature and humidity can also be factors. If the temperature is cold or the humidity is high, it takes longer for the mediums to dry so you have a longer working time as opposed to high heat and low humidity where you will need to work quickly. Also, if you are working on an absorbent surface, you will have to be quick, and if you are working on a non-porous surface, you will have more time.

You will get a feel for it after some experiments.

1 / PREPARE IMAGE AND BACKGROUND

Select an image. Using the ink-jet printer set to transparency, print the image onto the transparency. Using the paintbrush, apply a medium coat of soft gel to the background surface.

2 / PLACE IMAGE ONTO BACKGROUND

Place the transparency ink-side down onto the background. Be careful not to move the image.

TIP

Have you misplaced your brayer? Use your hand! Just make sure to apply an even pressure and cover all spots of the image.

3 / BRAYER IMAGE

Using the brayer, lightly smooth down the transparency to transfer the ink. Begin with a very light touch—especially if you have a thicker layer of soft gel. With your hand holding the transparency in place, lift a corner to check the transfer. If needed, place back the image down and apply more pressure with the brayer.

TROUBLESHOOTING

MY IMAGE WON'T TRANSFER

If not enough of the image is transferring, you may apply more pressure or mist the background with water. Remember to work quickly so your gel doesn't dry out.

TRANSPARENCY GLUED ON

WAITING BY THE WINDOW | *Transparency, blender pen transfers on painted and stamped background*

ARTWORK BY DARLENE OLIVIA McELROY

Materials ✳ toner-based or ink-jet printer ✳ transparency (dual use for both toner and ink-jet) ✳ scissors ✳ soft gel (gloss) or acrylic medium ✳ paintbrush or palette knife ✳ background surface ✳ brayer ✳ paper towel ✳ workable fixative for ink-jet transparencies

If you use multipurpose transparency film (for copiers, laser and ink-jet printers), you have more flexibility for all kinds of uses. This film is very clear and easily available. This technique can be done with either toner-based transparency or ink-jet. If using ink-jet you must spray it with a workable fixative prior to gluing it down.

LIMITATIONS

There is a visible edge, but it can be minimized with additional layers and finishes.

You're also limited to the standard size for transparencies: 8.5" × 11" (22cm × 28cm).

If using an acrylic medium, it takes a long time to dry and become clear.

SURFACE OPTIONS

Works well on canvas, panel, wood, paper and Plexiglas.

ARCHIVAL QUALITY

A toner-based image has a better quality than an ink-jet image, but UV-resistant gel or spray can help the quality.

NOTES

It is best to adhere the image printed-side down, so if you are printing text or music, you will need to print it using a mirror image or reverse.

Bold graphics work best, but experiment with all images.

TIP

You can get away from the super shiny finish of the transparency by putting a little clear gesso diluted with water over the surface and wiping off the excess. The gesso-water mixture can be anywhere from 20 percent water to half water, half gesso.

2 / CUT OUT IMAGE

Using the scissors, trim the image to the desired size.

1 / PREPARE IMAGE

Select an image. Using the printer, print it onto the rough side of the transparency. If using an ink-jet printer, let the printed transparency dry for about a half hour, then spray it with a workable fixative. If using a toner-based image, no workable fixative is necessary.

3 / APPLY MEDIUM

Determine the image placement on the background. Using the paintbrush or palette knife, apply soft gel or acrylic medium to the background.

★ TROUBLESHOOTING ★

THE IMAGE SMEARED. WHAT HAPPENED?

If the image smears when you brayer it to the surface, you probably forgot to use the spray fixative to set the image. Pull the transparency up and wipe away the gel so you can salvage the background. Then start over, making sure to use the spray fixative on the ink-jet image. If it still smears, consider using a toner-based transparency.

WHY ARE THERE AIR BUBBLES UNDER THE IMAGE?

This means there was not enough soft gel or medium used, and the image was not sufficiently smoothed out. If the background surface is textured at all, use a soft gel to fill in an uneven surface; use a polymer medium if the surface is smooth.

4 / LAY IMAGE ON BACKGROUND

Lay the image printed-side down onto the background.

5 / BRAYER IMAGE

Place the paper towel over the image. Using a brayer or your hand, smooth out the image to push out any air bubbles and adhere the image to the background. Let it dry flat. The acrylic is dry when it becomes clear; this may take several days. **29**

HEAT

Heat is used to transfer the imagery by baking it into a product, melting it, printing it or fusing it. Some products are made specifically for this purpose, like iron-on transfers, and others are unique, like using heat to fuse toner to plastic.

This section gives you ways to use transfers in jewelry, sculpting and sewing. Most of these methods use products in alternative ways or update older techniques. As we wrote this section, we kept asking ourselves what else could you stick a transfer onto. This is how we came up with the *Plastic Heat* technique (page 45). The *Fabric Crayons* (page 34) is fun to do with kids, and the *Liquid Polymer Skin* (page 43) and the *Polymer Clay* (page 48) techniques are great for jewelry and sculpture. *Fusible Web* (page 32) and *Iron-On Sheets* (page 41) are wonderful textile projects.

We also had some funny bloopers, like when we were experimenting with the fabric crayons, and we kept ironing and nothing was happening   only to discover the iron wasn't plugged in.

The instructions for these techniques are clear and easy to follow, but when working with hot surfaces, be sure to take the necessary precautions. Always use oven mitts when performing baking techniques, and never touch the hot surface of an iron or a heat tool. Follow the directions carefully, and allow all the transfer items to cool properly before handling them.

FUSIBLE WEB

Similar in texture to organza, this material will give you a soft diffused look. What's great is you don't need an adhesive, you just iron the transfer on to your background. When heating the material, it can develop holes giving it a distressed look, which has texture potential.

You can even try painting with watercolors on the fusible web.

LIMITATIONS
Soft fuzzy image, but you can increase the saturation of your image in your computer.

SURFACE OPTIONS
You can adhere it to fabric, aluminum foil, paper, wood or lightly painted, porous, acrylic surfaces.

You may need to glue the fusible web to surfaces you can't iron on or ones that are too textured.

ARCHIVAL QUALITY
Low to medium; UV-resistant spray or varnish finish will help with lightfastness.

NOTES
Let it dry completely at the end of step 2 to prevent smearing.

Make sure all of the fusible web's edges are adhered to the paper prior to printing; otherwise you could jam the printer.

THE GARDEN GATE | *Fusible web, acrylic paint and non-porous digital ground on aluminum foil.*
ARTWORK BY SANDRA DURAN WILSON

Materials ✳ ink-jet printer ✳ fusible web ✳ copy paper ✳ background surface ✳ tape ✳ iron ✳ towels or ironing board ✳ silicon sheet (optional) ✳ scissors ✳ workable fixative

Because the fusible web is heat-sensitive, you cannot iron this product onto freezer paper.

Don't use a brand new printer; use an everyday, workhorse printer. Follow steps 1 and 2 carefully to prevent paper jams in your printer.

Don't forget: The silicone sheet or backing paper helps prevent accidental fusing of fabrics or materials to your iron.

1 / PREPARE FUSIBLE WEB

Using the scissors, trim the fusible webbing (attached to its backing paper) slightly smaller than the copy paper. Remove the fusible web from its backing. Set the fusible backing aside to use later.

2 / PRINT IMAGE

Using the tape, secure the fusible web to the copy paper. Make sure the part that will feed through the printer is securely taped down. Run the fusible web through the ink-jet printer, making sure that the edges are taped and the webbing lies flat. Spray the printed image with the workable fixative. Let the image dry for a half hour.

3 / ADHERE IMAGE TO BACKGROUND

Using the scissors, cut out the desired fusible web image. Place the background surface on a towel or on the ironing board. Place the image onto the background surface. Place the fusible web backing over the image. If using the silicon sheet, place it on the surface of the art work. Place the thin towel over all the layers. Using the iron on a medium setting (no steam), adhere the image to the background by ironing over the towel.

TROUBLESHOOTING

WHY DID THE IMAGE SMEAR?

If the image is blurred, you did not spray it with a workable fixative. Be sure to spray it and let it dry before painting or sealing.

I LEFT THE BACKING ON. WHAT NOW?

If you leave the fusible paper backing on and run it through your printer, it tends to get wrinkled. If you like the look this provides, use it! If not, start with step 1 and be sure to remove the backing.

33

FABRIC CRAYONS

This is a fun and easy technique. You can build up textures and layers of fun drawings. It is also a great way to create a resist on a water-based painting.

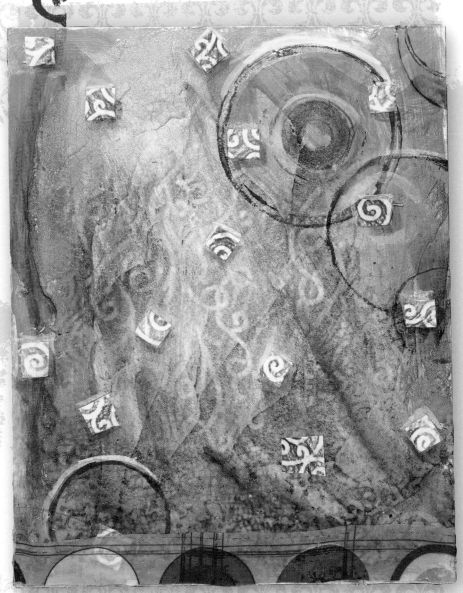

SPHERES OF LIGHT | *Fabric crayon transfer, light molding paste, collage and ExtravOrganza*

ARTWORK BY SANDRA DURAN WILSON

LIMITATIONS
You are limited to the colors from the box, but you can mix and blend.

SURFACE OPTIONS
This technique can work on fabric, water-based paintings, paper and wood.

ARCHIVAL QUALITY
Low, but may be improved using Krylon Preserve It! and a UV-resistant varnish.

NOTES
You can build up interesting patterns using different rubbing or textural surfaces with different colors.

You can also use a candle or regular crayon on the copy paper over texture and impart this to your painting as a resist.

Materials ❋ Crayola Fabric Crayons ❋ textured plates or surfaces ❋ background surface ❋ copy paper ❋ iron ❋ thin towels or paper towels ❋ silicone paper ❋ scissors ❋ paintbrush ❋ glue

1 / RUB IMAGE ONTO PAPER

Place a piece of copy paper over a textured plate or textured surface. Using a fabric crayon, rub over the surface. You can also blend another color on top.

2 / IRON IMAGE

If desired, prepare additional rubbings, and use the scissors to cut them to desired sizes. Set the background surface on the towel. Place the rubbings crayon side down onto the background, then place the silicone paper over the rubbing paper. Place a thin towel over the silicone paper. Using an iron on a medium setting (no steam), iron the transfer using gentle but firm pressure. Pull back a corner to see if the transfer is working.

3 / ADHERE IMAGE TO BACKGROUND

You may continue to iron other patterns onto the background until you have the desired results. When you are finished ironing, peel the image paper off the background. If desired, you can use the scissors to cut the image paper into shapes. Using a paintbrush, adhere the shapes to the background with a medium or glue of your choice.

★ TROUBLESHOOTING ★

I WAS USING A PAINTED BACKGROUND AND NOTHING SHOWED UP. WHAT HAPPENED?

We discovered that when trying this technique over an acrylic painting that the crayon didn't transfer as well. We then tried a wash—acrylic paint mixed with water—painted over the surface, and it acted as a resist. When we tried ironing the pattern again, it did show up.

I WAS USING A PAINTED BACKGROUND, AND IT MELTED. WHAT HAPPENED?

The heat from the iron can melt the paint if there is a thick layer. Try using a background that has a thinner layer of paint.

HEAT TOOL

We used a small round heat tool purchased from a craft supplier for this technique, but an iron you have at home will work just fine.

LIMITATIONS
It is harder to transfer large images because you can only heat a small area at a time, so there is a greater chance of the toner copy moving and becoming blurry. This technique also doesn't work well with textured surfaces.

SURFACE OPTIONS
This technique works best on paper, glass, metal and wood. It will also work on Plexiglas, but it can warp the surface. It's not recommended for paintings because it may melt the surface if the paint application is too thick.

ARCHIVAL QUALITY
The quality is high, but we always recommend a UV-resistant coating.

NOTES
This technique is great for text on Plexiglas. Remember when you use this technique that the image will be reversed unless you adjust the orientation when you make the copy.

THE FUN ZONE | *Heat tool transfer, direct gel transfer, blender pen transfer and embellishments*
ARTWORK BY DARLENE OLIVIA McELROY

Materials ✳ **toner-based image** ✳ **background surface** ✳ **heat transfer tool** ✳ **tape**

1 / PLACE IMAGE ON BACKGROUND

Print a color or black-and-white toner-based image. Place the image toner-side down onto the background. Using the tape, secure the image to the background.

2 / APPLY HEAT

Using the heat tool, slowly make small circular motions on the paper.

3 / CHECK TRANSFER

Lift a section of the image's back to check the transfer. Repeat step 2 until the desired transfer is achieved.

★ TROUBLESHOOTING ★

THE PAPER GOT BURNED. IS THAT OK?

If you hold the heat transfer tool in one spot for too long, the paper will burn, making the image harder to transfer. Use a slow, steady pressure and small circular motions. You can come back to a spot that hasn't transferred well.

I WAS WORKING ON A PAINTED SURFACE AND MADE A MESS. WHAT HAPPENED?

Your paint layer is too thick. If you're going to transfer onto a painted background, make it a thin layer, and don't heat in one place for too long. You can go back over the spot later if you need to.

HOMEMADE INK-JET FABRIC

This is an inexpensive way to make your own cotton, canvas, organza or silk fabric transfers. You can get interesting combinations with different fabrics and patterns.

You may use your fabric in many different ways, like quilting, stretching on stretcher bars, painting it and experimenting with other fabrics.

SPRING LOVE | *Ink-jet fabric transfers, encaustic papers and collage.*
ARTWORK BY SANDRA DURAN WILSON

LIMITATIONS
This technique does not work well with synthetic fabrics. Size is limited to the size of your printer feed.

SURFACE OPTIONS
You can sew fabrics or glue them on to most surfaces.

ARCHIVAL QUALITY
Low to medium but can be enhanced with a UV-resistant spray.

NOTES
This technique does not work with toner-based copiers and printers.

The image will be reproduced backwards, but it can be flipped or make a mirror image in your computer.

Let it dry completely in step 2 to prevent smearing.

Make sure all edges are stuck to the paper prior to printing, otherwise you may get a paper jam. Even when ironing in step 1, it may be best to tape the corners to prevent a paper jam.

Don't use your brand new printer; use your everyday workhorse printer.

Use a regular paper setting not the photo setting.

Materials ✳ ink-jet printer ✳ natural fabric ✳ background surface ✳ copy paper ✳ freezer or butcher paper ✳ iron ✳ towel ✳ scissors ✳ workable fixative ✳ polymer medium or soft gel (gloss) ✳ cellophane tape ✳ paintbrush

1 / PREPARE FABRIC

Using the scissors, trim the fabric and the butcher or freezer paper about 1/4" (6mm), smaller than the copy paper. Place the fabric on top of the glossy side of the butcher or freezer paper. Place the towel over the fabric. Using the iron on a medium setting (no steam), iron the layers using a steady pressure. Lift a corner of the towel, and check the fabric paper adhesion.

2 / PRINT IMAGE TO FABRIC

Check the edge of the fabric and secure it with the cellophane tape if necessary. Select an image. Using the manual feed option on the ink-jet printer, print the image onto the fabric. If you accidentally print on the butcher paper, simply turn it over and reprint. Let the image dry for about 15 minutes. Peel the fabric from the butcher or freezer paper. Spray the image with the workable fixative.

3 / CUT IMAGE

Allow the image to dry thoroughly. If desired, use scissors to cut out the image.

4 / APPLY MEDIUM TO BACKGROUND

Using the paintbrush, apply the polymer medium or soft gel onto the background surface.

5 / ADHERE IMAGE TO BACKGROUND

Place the fabric on top of the background. Using the paintbrush, smooth the image down with the polymer medium or soft gel to adhere it to the background.

★ TROUBLESHOOTING ★

WHO NEEDS TO IRON? YOU DO!

Do yourself a favor and don't skip the ironing. If you only tape the fabric down, it will most likely end up a crumpled mess in your printer. If you do jam your printer, gently extract the sheet and clean up any strings or paper pieces.

I WAS PAINTING OVER MY IMAGE AND IT SMEARED. WHAT HAPPENED?

If the image is blurred when painting over it in step 5, you most likely didn't spray it with the workable fixative. Stop as soon as you see it is smearing. Let the medium dry, and spray it with the fixative again. Let it set for a half hour, and then try to affix it with acrylic medium or glue.

40

IRON-ON SHEETS

We use ink-jet t-shirt iron-on transfer sheets that can be found at fabric and office supply stores. We find that brands vary.

THROUGH THE WINDOW | *Iron-on transfer, papers and stamps*
ARTWORK BY DARLENE OLIVIA McELROY

LIMITATIONS
The transfer size is limited to the size of the printer feed. This technique doesn't work well on acrylic painted surfaces. Using a heat transfer on an acrylic painted surface tends to make the surface mushy.

SURFACE OPTIONS
This technique works well with fabric, papers, aluminum foil, lightly painted surfaces and wood veneers.

ARCHIVAL QUALITY
Medium, but UV-resistant sprays will improve archival quality.

NOTES
This is a fun technique to use with patterned fabrics, specialty papers and aluminum foil.

This technique will work over watercolor paintings.

Materials ✳ ink-jet printer ✳ t-shirt iron-on transfer paper ✳ background surface ✳ iron ✳ paper towel ✳ scissors

41

1 / PREPARE IMAGE

Using the ink-jet printer, print the selected image onto the iron-on transfer paper following the manufacturer's directions. If desired, use the scissors to cut out the image.

2 / PLACE IMAGE ON BACKGROUND

Place the image printed-side down onto the background surface.

3 / IRON IMAGE

Place a paper towel over the transfer sheet. Iron the image according to the manufacturer's directions.

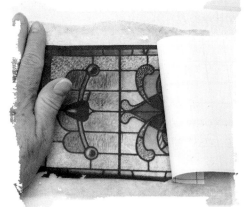

4 / CHECK TRANSFER

Peel the backing to check the transfer. If needed, iron more. When you are satisfied with the transfer, peel the backing off while it is still hot.

★ TROUBLESHOOTING ★

MY IMAGE DIDN'T TRANSFER VERY WELL. CAN I FIX IT?

First, check the iron. Is it hot enough? If not, be sure it's on the right setting and let it heat up more. If the heat setting is OK, place the transfer back very carefully, matching the holes as best you can, and iron some more.

OOPS, I PRINTED THE IMAGE ON THE WRONG SIDE!

That's OK. If you have accidentally printed on the wrong side, send the transfer sheet through your printer again on the correct side.

42

LIQUID POLYMER SKIN

This technique works with toner-based or magazine images. The flexibility of this skin is great for making dimensional shapes like beads or sculptural objects.

We recommend having a toaster oven dedicated to baking liquid polymers and clays. Garage sales are a great place to find them. As some ovens run hotter, we recommend getting an oven thermometer to get an accurate temperature reading.

LIMITATIONS
The size of the craft or toaster oven and its heat distribution can limit this technique.

If adhering the polymer skin to another object, there will be a visible edge.

SURFACE OPTIONS
Use a glue to adhere the skin to canvas, panel and papers. You can also form the skin into beads and other dimensional shapes.

ARCHIVAL QUALITY
Medium to high.

NOTES
Some ovens have an uneven heating temperature. One area might be burned and another not baked enough. You might have to experiment with the ovens and the image's placement on the rack.

FEELING LIKE ROYALTY | *Liquid polymer transfer, rhinestone crown and embellishments*
ARTWORK BY DARLENE OLIVIA McELROY

Materials ✳ toner-based or magazine image ✳ background surface ✳ liquid polymer ✳ paintbrush ✳ sandpaper ✳ craft oven or toaster oven dedicated to craft projects ✳ ceramic tile or baking sheet ✳ spray bottle with water ✳ soft gel (gloss) or polymer medium (gloss)

1 / APPLY LIQUID POLYMER TO IMAGE

Choose a magazine or toner-based image. Using the paintbrush, apply the liquid polymer to the image.

2 / BAKE IMAGE

Place the image onto a ceramic tile or baking sheet polymer-side up, and place the into the oven. Bake the image at 250–300°F (121–149°C) for approximately 15–30 minutes. Allow it to cool thoroughly. Using the sandpaper, lightly roughen up the back of the paper.

3 / MOISTEN IMAGE BACKING

Using the spray bottle with water, moisten the paper backing.

4 / RUB OFF BACKING

Using your fingers, rub off the backing to reveal the image. Steps 3 and 4 may have to be repeated several times to remove all the paper backing. If adhering to a background, use polymer medium or soft gel as a glue.

TROUBLESHOOTING

WHY DOES MY LIQUID POLYMER SKIN HAVE BUBBLES?

This happened to us, and it was a neat effect, but not what we wanted. It is possible your bottle of liquid polymer may be really old. Check the date on the bottle. The consistency of older liquid polymer is different from fresh.

Another explanation: It may have been baked at too high a temperature or for too long. Next time check it every few minutes toward the end of the baking time.

THIS PAPER IS REALLY DIFFICULT TO TAKE OFF.

Pat the image dry, then bake the liquid polymer a little longer. Just don't bake it too long, or you'll get the bubbles mentioned above!

PLASTIC HEAT

This transfer technique uses heat to fuse the toner-based image or magazine image to the plastic, making a very thin, skin-like image. It's crisp, and you don't need to reverse images for direction such as letters.

LIMITATIONS

This technique is harder to transfer to large areas.

SURFACE OPTIONS

It glues to almost anything.

ARCHIVAL QUALITY

Medium to high; UV-resistant gels and sprays add to its archival quality.

NOTES

Choose a heavily inked color image—the plastic wrap will not stick to any white areas because there is no ink.

If you adhere the transfer to a background surface, apply clear acrylic before laying it down to help it become more clear.

Instead of an iron, you can use a heat gun, but it takes more care as it may burn holes in the plastic wrap. An iron also makes the image flatter.

This transfer can be sewn easily.

TIP

If you're using a heat gun, tape the plastic wrap to the image surface and use slow, steady heat. If you are heavy handed, the plastic wrap tends to get burn holes.

HAND ME DOWN | *Dress made with muslin, stencils and plastic heat transfer*
ARTWORK BY DARLENE OLIVIA McELROY

Materials ✳ toner-based or magazine image ✳ plastic wrap ✳ iron ✳ sandpaper ✳ spray bottle with water ✳ silicone paper ✳ thin towels ✳ scissors

1 / PREPARE IMAGE

Place the chosen image on the towel. Tear a piece of plastic wrap from the roll so it is larger than the picture. Using the scissors, trim off any excess plastic wrap. Using your hands, smooth the plastic wrap over the image.

2 / LAYER SILICONE PAPER AND TOWEL

Place the silicone paper over the plastic wrap. Make sure the plastic doesn't go beyond the silicone sheet, or it may stick to the towel. Place the thin towel over the silicone paper.

★ TROUBLESHOOTING ★

WHY WON'T THE PLASTIC WRAP STICK TO THE PICTURE?

Sometimes, it's just a matter of patience; keep ironing! This process may take some time, and in our experience, edges can take the longest to stick.

Another explanation is that there is too much white in the image. This technique works best with heavily inked images because the plastic wrap needs something to bond with—white space has nothing for it to stick to.

3 / IRON IMAGE

Using the iron on a medium-high heat setting (no steam), apply heat in a slow and steady manner to the towel.

4 / CHECK TRANSFER

Periodically, peel back the top towel and silicone sheet to check for adherence.

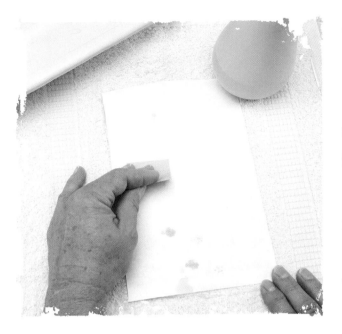

5 / SAND BACKING

When you are satisfied with the transfer, let the project cool (don't forget to turn off the iron). Using the scissors, trim off any excess plastic. Using the sandpaper, lightly roughen up the back of the image.

6 / SATURATE IMAGE WITH WATER

Using the spray bottle with water, wet the back of the image with water. You could also place the image in a tray of water to saturate the paper.

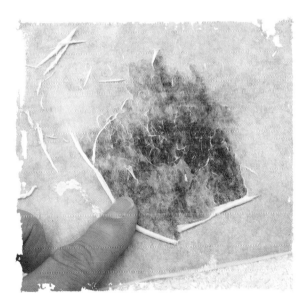

★ TROUBLESHOOTING ★

7 / REMOVE PAPER BACKING

Using your fingers or a soft cloth, rub the paper off the back. Spray with water as needed. You may have to repeat steps 6 and 7 to get all the paper residue off. Allow the picture to dry thoroughly before embellishing.

TIP

To keep the paper from curling while drying after step 7, place the transfer between paper towels and blot it. Smooth it out using your hands and let it dry between the paper towels.

I RUBBED OFF PART OF THE IMAGE! WHAT HAPPENED?

Keep the following in mind for the next time. Carefully check that the plastic and the image are bonded before sanding. If they are not, it will be easier to rub the image off. Also, don't rub too hard in step 7. You can repeat that step several times to take off the layers of paper. If you press too hard while rubbing, you will likely take some of the image off.

Of course, you may consider this a happy mistake. Perhaps the small hole adds a distressed element to your final artwork. You can also sand the back of an image to give it a distressed look.

POLYMER CLAY

This transfer works with magazine images and toner-based images.

We recommend having a toaster oven dedicated for baking liquid polymers and clays. Garage sales are a great place to find them. As some ovens run hotter, we recommend getting an oven thermometer to get an accurate temperature reading.

LIMITATIONS

The color of the polymer clay will affect your image, as the lighter areas of the toner-based or magazine image will be transparent when the transfer is made. Any white areas of the image will be transparent, resulting in the color of the clay showing through.

SURFACE OPTIONS

Polymer clay comes in many colors plus you can adjust the color of your image in your computer to make interesting combinations.

ARCHIVAL QUALITY

Medium. We recommend a UV-resistant varnish or spray on the completed piece to improve the archival quality.

NOTES

In addition to creating elements to put in your art pieces or art books, this technique can be used for jewelry and sculpture.

BALANCING DANGER | *Polymer clay transfer, blender marker, stamps and found objects*
ARTWORK BY DARLENE OLIVIA McELROY

Materials ✳ toner-based or magazine image ✳ polymer clay ✳ craft oven or toaster oven ✳ rolling pin or can

1 / PREPARE IMAGE

Condition the polymer clay according to the package directions. Using the rolling pin or can, roll out the polymer clay to about ¼" (6mm) thick. A thicker clay may affect the baking time. Place the image facedown on the clay. Using your hands, smooth the image down.

2 / BAKE IMAGE

In the craft oven, bake the clay for approximately 15–30 minutes at 250–300°F (121–130°C). When it's finished baking, remove the clay and let it cool. Peel the paper off the clay to reveal the transfer.

★ TROUBLESHOOTING ★

THE CLAY WAS BAKED TOO LONG. DOES THAT MATTER?

When the clay is baked too long, the paper will burn. The paper will most likely stick to the clay, so you'll see more paper than the image. We recommend using a timer to remind you to remove the project.

WHY DIDN'T MY PICTURE TRANSFER?

If you check the transfer and it looks like the above photo, you probably didn't bake the clay long enough. Smooth the image back down and bake a little longer.

49

SOLVENTS

The techniques in this section use solvents, which are usually clear liquids that have characteristic odors. Solvents change the make-up of the original image, breaking it down and allowing the image to transfer. This section is by far the smelliest, but we've found that the wide range of transfer surface options make up for the odors. We chose these techniques because no specialized equipment is required. We did extensive experiments with some techniques to explore reasons why they wouldn't work.

If you want to transfer onto anything from rocks to Plexiglas, try the Lazertran techniques using polymer medium (page 64) or turpentine (page 67). *Crystal Clear* is an easy way to transfer high-contrast images (page 55), while *Wintergreen Oil* (page 75) makes beautiful color transfers. *Blender Marker* (page 52) is one of our students' favorite transfers and the *Preserve It* (page 70) is an inexpensive way to make your own rub-on transfers.

The majority of these techniques include great troubleshooting sections, as solvent transfers can be some of the trickiest techniques to achieve. Since these techniques all have strong odors (except for Gum Arabic), be sure to use the solvents with care and in well-ventilated areas.

BLENDER MARKER

Blender markers are a convenient method of storing and applying xylene. You can do this using the chemical and a brush, but the packaged markers are easier, less messy and emit less fumes. Make sure you get the xylene blender markers, as this technique will not work with alcohol markers.

We recommend the Chartpak AD Marker Blender.

LIMITATIONS
You should probably stay away from this if you are chemically sensitive. Although it says it is non-toxic, use this in a well-ventilated area. Larger sizes are more difficult, and smellier, to transfer.

SURFACE OPTIONS
This technique can work on paper, matte painted surfaces, metal, glass, Plexiglas, Sculpey/Fimo and rocks.

ARCHIVAL QUALITY
Low to medium. These transfers can be maintained using a UV-resistant spray after the image has dried.

NOTES
It is best to work in small areas and burnish rather than try to work on a large area all at once. Because a magazine is printed on both sides, it might be better to make a copy of the magazine image to avoid a mess.

Images using this technique will be reproduced backwards, but you can flip the image when making copies to ensure words read in the correct direction.

WELCOME HOME | *Rice paper, gampi tissue and embellishments transfers over fiber medium and painted background*
ARTWORK BY SANDRA DURAN WILSON

Materials ✳ toner-based or magazine image ✳ blender marker ✳ ✳ gampi paper or rice paper ✳ background surface ✳ acrylic medium (gloss) or soft gel (gloss) ✳ burnisher ✳ paintbrush ✳ scissors ✳ tape

Also, blender markers transfer colors in the reverse order of how they were printed, which makes yellows in the image the most difficult to reproduce.

1 / CUT OUT IMAGE

Select an image. Using the scissors, cut out the image, leaving a border.

2 / APPLY BLENDER MARKER

Place the image toner-side down onto the gampi or rice paper (here we've used gampi paper). Using the tape, secure one side of the paper to the surface. Using the blender marker, go over small sections of the image.

3 / BURNISH SMALL SECTIONS

Using the burnishing tool, such ass scissor handles, immediately burnish hard the small section where you just applied the blender marker.

TIP

When cutting out the image, be sure to leave a border; this will allow you to tape down the image and not hinder the transfer.

4 / CHECK TRANSFER

Lift the paper to check the transfer. Repeat steps 2 and 3 to cover the entire image. Keep the image taped to the background until you are happy with the transfer.

5 / APPLY ADHESIVE TO BACKGROUND

Using the paintbrush, apply the polymer medium or soft gel onto the background surface.

6 / ADHERE IMAGE

Place the paper with the image onto the background surface, and apply the polymer medium or soft gel over the image to seal it.

TROUBLESHOOTING

I'M WORKING ON A NON-POROUS SURFACE, AND MY TRANSFER IS MUDDY. WHAT HAPPENED?

When using this technique on a smooth surface, such as Plexiglas or metal, it can be very easy for the image to smear. Why? Because you don't need to use as much xylene solution or to burnish as hard as you would on a rough or porous surface. Use a lighter touch when burnishing on smooth surfaces, and check the image transfer often; you can always go back over it if the transfer is too light.

WHY IS MY TRANSFER SO LIGHT?

If you decided to use the blender marker on large sections of the paper, the marker will dry and the image will transfer too lightly or not at all. Stick to using 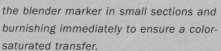 *the blender marker in small sections and burnishing immediately to ensure a color-saturated transfer.*

WILL THIS TECHNIQUE WORK ON AN ACRYLIC BACKGROUND?

This technique can work on acrylics. Two things you should remember when using this technique with acrylic backgrounds: You need to use a thin coat of acrylics and a light touch when burnishing. If the acrylic layer is too thick, it can become gummy when being burnished, and the image will be distorted or won't transfer.

CRYSTAL CLEAR

This technique works with black-and-white and color toner-based images on a variety of surfaces. You must use a lighter touch with the burnishing when working on non-absorbent surfaces.

Timing is critical in this technique, so be sure to follow the directions closely to ensure a good transfer.

THE STROLL | *Crystal Clear transfer, blender marker transfer, stamped images and embellishments*
ARTWORK BY DARLENE OLIVIA McELROY

LIMITATIONS
You should probably stay away from this if you are chemically sensitive.

SURFACE OPTIONS
Paper, paint, metal, Plexiglas, glass and wood.

ARCHIVAL QUALITY
High, but we always recommend finishing a piece with a UV-resistant gel or spray coating.

NOTES
Work in a well ventilated area.
For best results, use a high-contrast image.

Materials ✳ toner-based image ✳ background surface ✳
Krylon Crystal Clear ✳ bone folder or large spoon

1 / SPRAY FRONT OF IMAGE

Choose an image. Spray the front of the toner-based image generously with the Crystal Clear.

2 / TONER WILL RISE ON FRONT

The toner will rise on the front of the image. You may need to hold the paper at an angle to see the raised ink.

3 / IMAGE WILL SHOW THROUGH BACK

The image will begin to show on the back of the paper.

4 / BURNISH IMAGE

While the paper is still wet, place the image toner-side down onto the background surface. Using the bone folder or a large spoon, rub the image onto the background surface.

5 / CHECK TRANSFER

Peel the image back to check that it is transferring. You may have to spray it again and burnish if there are weak areas.

TROUBLESHOOTING

WHY IS MY TRANSFER LIGHTER IN SOME PLACES?

Lighter areas, as seen below, can happen for two reasons.

You did not use enough Crystal Clear. Refer to steps 2 and 3 to get the right amount.

If you wait too long before burnishing the Crystal Clear will set the image, Once that happens, you'll have to start the process over. Be quick to burnish the image after spraying it with Crystal Clear.

Of course, this could add a little more texture to your finished art piece. But if you really want a solid transfer, burnish immediately.

WHY IS MY IMAGE MUDDY?

Here are the two most common reasons:

The image in the transfer shown above doesn't have a lot of contrast, which resulted in a poor transfer. To avoid this, always use a high-contrast image.

You used too much Crystal Clear. Remember, you should be able to see the image from the back, but it shouldn't be soaking wet!

GAMPI/SILK TISSUE

This transfer, which works with both toner-based and ink-jet printers, is one of the most popular methods we teach. The silk tissue virtually disappears when you adhere it with a little diluted polymer gloss. This technique allows you to create collages without a paper edge.

The trickiest part is getting it to print and not jam your printer. Carefully follow step 1 for so you have no problems.

LIMITATIONS
The size of the printer paper feed limits the size of the image.

SURFACE OPTIONS
You can adhere this to most surfaces.

ARCHIVAL QUALITY
The quality is higher with a toner-based copier than with an ink-jet printer. We recommend finishing with a UV-resistant spray to improve the archival quality of both types.

NOTES
Gampi tissue can be applied over heavy textures, which makes it more versatile than most transfers.

Mix polymer with a dab of water for a clearer background (unprinted tissue will almost disappear).

BUDDHA AND THE BURNING BUSH | *Ink-jet gampi transfer, paint, encaustic printmaking and embellishments*

ARTWORK BY SANDRA DURAN WILSON

Materials ✳ gampi or silk tissue ✳ scissors ✳ tape ✳ copy paper ✳ ✳ printer ✳ background surface ✳ workable fixative (for ink-jet image only) ✳ ✳ polymer medium (gloss) or soft gel (gloss) ✳ paintbrush

1 / PREPARE GAMPI OR SILK TISSUE

Using the scissors, trim the gampi or the silk tissue ¼"
(6mm) smaller than the copy paper. Using the tape, secure
the gampi/silk tissue to the piece of copy paper.

2 / PREPARE IMAGE

Using the printer of your choice, print the image onto
the tissue by using the printer's manual paper feed.

If using an image from an ink-jet printer, spray the
image with the workable fixative after printing it. Allow it to
dry thoroughly.

3 / APPLY MEDIUM TO SURFACE

Using the paintbrush, apply the polymer medium or the soft gel
to the background.

TIP
You can also iron the Gampi onto freezer paper
that is cut to the size of a piece of copy paper.

4 / APPLY IMAGE TO BACKGROUND

Remove the gampi or silk tissue image from the
copy paper. Remove the tape. Place the image onto
the background surface. Using the paintbrush, brush
the image with the polymer medium or soft gel to
adhere the image to the background.

GUM ARABIC

Gum arabic transfers are also known as paper plate lithography. It is a little more technical but worth the effort. You can create your own background papers or use photographs or other favorite imagery. Your black-and-white toner copy becomes your litho plate.

THROUGH THE WINDOW | *Gum arabic transfers, stamps and embellishments*
ARTWORK BY DARLENE OLIVIA McELROY

LIMITATIONS
This process can be done using a spoon or burnisher, but the process works best with a printing press. The size is limited by copier size.

SURFACE OPTIONS
Absorbent papers like rice papers, watercolor paper (smooth), canvas, natural fabric or print papers.

ARCHIVAL QUALITY
High.

NOTES
If using a watercolor or printmaking paper, you should mist them with water prior to transferring the image.

Do not use recycled copy paper because it falls apart.

The image will print in reverse, so if the image includes words or numbers, make the necessary adjustments when you print or make a copy.

For a quick cleanup use baby oil to clean the tools and Plexiglas. Wash them thoroughly with soap and water, and let them dry completely.

Toner-based images from a copier work better than those printed from a laser printer.

Materials ✳ high-contrast, black-and-white toner-based image ✳ background surface ✳ gum arabic ✳ piece of Plexiglas ✳ palette or sheet of wax paper ✳ oil paints (opaque paints work best) ✳ linseed oil ✳ scrap paper ✳ palette knife ✳ brayer ✳ sponge ✳ small container of water ✳ printmaking or watercolor paper ✳ pasta machine or large spoon ✳ plastic bag ✳ scissors ✳ thin piece of soft foam (pasta machine only)

1 / PREPARE PAPER AND IMAGE

If you are using the pasta machine: Using the scissors, cut the paper you are transferring to and the black-and-white image to fit through the rollers.

If you are using the spoon to burnish: You are only restricted by the size of the photocopy. Trim the paper to any size you like, or keep the sheet intact.

2 / MIX PAINTS

Using the spray bottle, mist the printmaking paper or watercolor paper with water and seal it inside the plastic bag to keep it damp. (Thin rice papers should not be misted.)

Using the palette (you can use a sheet of wax paper) and the palette knife, mix the oil paints with a drop or two of linseed oil until smooth. The paint should be buttery not sticky. Take some of the paint and put onto the palette. Roll the brayer back and forth through the paint until it is loaded with paint, then set it aside.

3 / SMOOTH IMAGE ON PLEXIGLAS

Pour a small amount of the gum arabic on the Plexiglas. Using a damp sponge with a small amount of gum arabic on it, wipe down the area on the Plexiglas where you will lay the image. Place the image on that spot toner-side up. Using the damp sponge, smooth out any wrinkles. Pick up some gum arabic with the sponge and begin to work it into the image until it is gummy and saturated. Try to work in one direction.

4 / APPLY PAINT TO IMAGE

Using the loaded brayer, and starting from the center, apply a layer of paint to the image. Work only in one direction, not back and forth.

5 / WIPE OFF INK

Using the damp sponge, mix some water and a small amount of gum arabic, and begin to gently wipe the paint off the paper. The paint will stay in the black areas and wipe off the light areas. Have the small container of water nearby so you can occasionally rinse the sponge.

6 / LAY IMAGE ONTO DAMP PAPER

Take the damp printmaking or watercolor paper out of the bag. Lay the image facedown onto the paper.

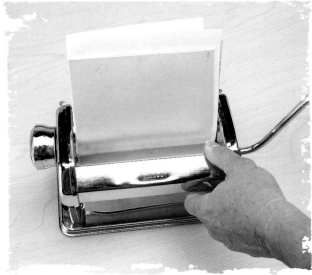

TIP

An alternative way to remove paint is to hold the painted copy over a tray and spray it with water until the paint is off the light areas.

7 / RUN THROUGH PASTA MACHINE

If you are using the pasta machine: Fold the piece of scrap paper around the image and the paper. Set the pasta machine on its tightest setting. Using the thin piece of soft foam to add tension, run the papers through the pasta machine.

8 / BURNISH WITH SPOON

If you are burnishing by hand. Place the image and the paper onto the piece of scrap paper. Using the spoon, burnish the image onto the paper.

9 / REMOVE PAPER

Pull the paper off to check the transfer.

TROUBLESHOOTING

TOO MUCH WATER AND THE PAPER WILL TEAR.

In step 5, if you slop the water on, the paper will become mushy and tear. It's best to dip the sponge into the water, then squeeze out any excess water. You want the sponge to be damp, not wet.

THE PAINT DOESN'T SEEM RIGHT. HOW CAN I FIX IT?

When mixing the paint in step 2, you want the consistency of the paint to be buttery, not sticky or slippery.

If the paint is slippery, you've added too much of the linseed oil. To fix this, add more paint a little at a time until the mixture reaches a buttery consistency. Be sure to mix well after each addition of paint.

If the paint mixture is too sticky, then you've added too much paint. Add more linseed oil, a bit at a time, and mix well until you reach the right consistency.

WHY DIDN'T MY IMAGE TRANSFER?

If the image transfer is too light, there are two possible explanations. First, the pasta machine press isn't tight enough or you didn't burnish enough. If this is the case, repeat step 7 if you are using a pasta machine, or step 8 if you are burnishing by hand.

If the image has been thoroughly burnished, perhaps the copy quality is bad. The success of this transfer depends on the toner-based copy. We find older copiers put more toner on the paper. If your transfer results using your home printer or copier are poor, try a print shop; you can test images from different machines and increase the toner if necessary.

LAZERTRAN WITH POLYMER MEDIUM

SEA OF LIFE | *Lazertran with polymer transfer painted over with an alcohol dissolve*
ARTWORK BY SANDRA DURAN WILSON

Materials ❋ ink-jet printer ❋ Lazertran for ink-jet ❋ background surface ❋ polymer medium (gloss) ❋ oil based varnish (optional) ❋ paintbrush ❋ tray of warm water ❋ paper towels

This technique gives you very crisp transfers onto paper, paintings, Plexiglas, glass, metal, wood and almost anything else. Be sure you buy the correct Lazertran for your printer.

The Lazertran attached with the polymer medium can be repositioned, so if you find you have put it in the wrong place you can carefully move it. This is not so with the turpentine application (see page 67).

The background will be white when the image dries. You can render it transparent with the optional step of applying an oil-based varnish on top.

LIMITATIONS
Because this is an emulsion transfer and you are using a polymer medium to put it on the surface, there will be a slight edge and plastic feel. Using soft gel on top will make the edge disappear somewhat.

SURFACE OPTIONS
This technique works well on almost anything.

ARCHIVAL QUALITY
Low to medium, but can be enhanced with a UV-resistant spray.

NOTES
If you wish to make a larger image than the size of the Lazertran, you can resize the image with Photoshop or another software program and print it on several sheets. This is known as tiling.

When the transfer has completely dried, you can sand it for an aged look.

Do not get the Lazertran sheet wet prior to use, as it glues the emulsion to the paper backing, and won't let the image slide off.

If the Lazertran is old, it will need a longer soaking time.

You can print a lot of small images onto a sheet of Lazertran so there is no wasted space.

1 / PREPARE IMAGE

Using the ink-jet printer, print the image onto the Lazertran paper. In the tray of warm water, place the image facedown. In the tray of warm water, place the image facedown. Let the image rest until the transfer sheet starts to release from the backing.

2 / BLOT IMAGE

Place the Lazertran with the image on the paper towel and blot well. Be gentle! Lazertran is fragile.

TROUBLESHOOTING

3 / APPLY POLYMER MEDIUM TO BACKGROUND

Using the paintbrush, apply a thin layer of the polymer medium onto the background surface.

HOW DO I KNOW WHEN THE PAPER IS READY?

The paper and the transfer sheet will start to separate. You can test the paper by lightly sliding the transfer sheet from the paper backing; if it moves, it's ready.

If you see white spots on the back side, that is where the transfer sheet is still stuck to the paper. Older Lazertran will be more fragile and take longer to release from the paper backing.

4 / TRANSFER IMAGE TO BACKGROUND

Holding the bottom edge of the Lazertran with the paintbrush, slide the Lazertran backing out from under the top layer.

5 / ADHERE IMAGE

Using a clean, damp paintbrush, smooth out any air pockets by making a cross through the image and working out in a radial pattern. Allow the image to dry thoroughly.

If your transfer is to be opaque: use a paintbrush and apply polymer medium over the image. If you want the image to be transparent: follow step 6.

6 / OPTIONAL STEP: TRANSPARENCY

If you desire transparency and want to show the surface color and texture underneath the image, apply 2 or 3 coats of any oil-based varnish with a clean paintbrush. Allow the image to dry between coats. This step may have to be repeated several times to achieve the desired transparency. Do not brush over with polymer medium.

LAZERTRAN WITH TURPENTINE

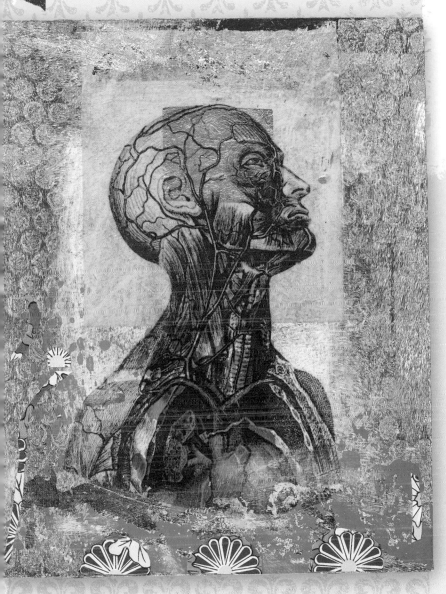

NATURE THOUGHTS | *Lazertran with turpentine transfer, collage elements and gold leaf on painted surface*

ARTWORK BY DARLENE OLIVIA McELROY

Materials ✳ ink-jet printer ✳ Lazertran for ink-jet ✳ background surface ✳ turpentine ✳ oil-based varnish ✳ scissors ✳ paper towels ✳ paintbrush ✳ tray of warm water

This technique gives you very crisp transfers onto almost any surface.

When using an ink-jet printer, the background will be white when the image dries. This technique renders the background transparent.

To draw on top of the Lazertran image or it use it as a barrier between multiple turpentine transfers, use a clear gesso to seal the image and give the surface tooth.

LIMITATIONS
Old Lazertran or too much turpentine when applied can cause the image to break up. Older Lazertran is also difficult to reposition once it has touched the background surface.

Any water left on the image after blotting will leave a pocket where the image is not adhered.

SURFACE OPTIONS
This technique works on almost any surface.

ARCHIVAL QUALITY
Low to medium; UV-resistant spray is always recommended.

NOTES
You must use real turpentine; alternatives will not work.

Be sure to use warm water for this technique; it will take the transfer sheet longer to release from the paper backing if you use cold water.

When the transfer has completely dried, try sanding it for an aged look.

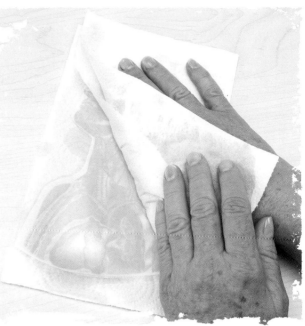

1 / PREPARE IMAGE

Choose an image. Using the ink-jet printer, print the image onto the Lazertran paper. Let the image dry for a half hour. If desired, use scissors to cut out the image. In the tray of warm water, place the image facedown. Let the image rest until the transfer sheet starts to release from the backing.

2 / BLOT IMAGE

Place the Lazertran image on the paper towel and blot well.

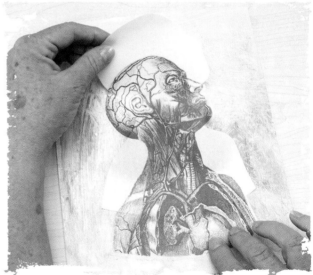

3 / APPLY TURPENTINE TO BACKGROUND SURFACE

Using the paintbrush, apply a thin layer of the turpentine onto the background.

4 / APPLY IMAGE TO BACKGROUND

Holding the bottom edge of the Lazertran, slide the Lazertran backing out from under the top layer.

TIP

If you're worried about using too much turpentine, try patting the transfer smooth with your hands instead of applying more turpentine in step 5. Make sure your hands are clean and dry when you begin, and thoroughly wash them when you are finished.

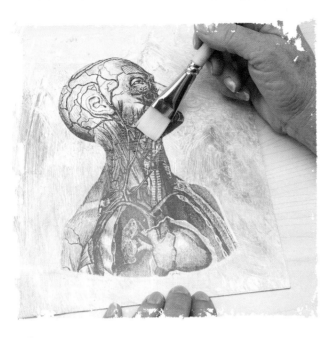

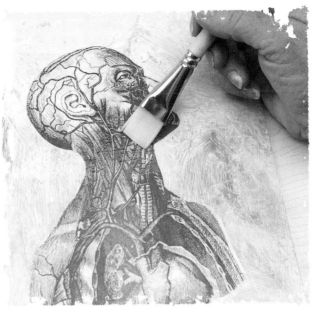

5 / SMOOTH IMAGE

Using the clean, damp paintbrush, smooth out any air pockets by making a cross through the image and working out in a radial pattern with the remaining turpentine on the brush. Do this carefully.

6 / APPLY VARNISH

Allow the image to dry. Using a clean paintbrush, apply 2–3 coats of any oil-based varnish, allowing the artwork to dry between applications.

TROUBLESHOOTING

WHY IS MY IMAGE DISSOLVING?

If the image is breaking up, you probably have too much turpentine on either your background or the brush. It's best to start by applying the turpentine sparingly, and adding only what is necessary for the image to adhere to the background.

WHY IS IT TAKING A LONG TIME FOR THE LAZERTRAN TRANSFER TO COME OFF THE BACKING?

There are three possible reasons for this: the Lazertran is old, the water is too cold or the Lazertran got wet and then dried.

Be sure to use warm water for this technique; it will take the transfer sheet longer to release from the paper backing if you use cold water. There is no way to tell if the Lazertran is too old.

WHY ISN'T MY LAZERTRAN IMAGE BECOMING CLEAR?

You probably forgot to apply the oil-based varnish on top of the image. Be sure the image is thoroughly dry before you put it on.

69

PRESERVE IT

TIME TARGET | *Preserve It! transfer, gum arabic print and collage*
ARTWORK BY SANDRA DURAN WILSON

This method is a homemade version of a transparency transfer. It is a simple and quick way to get a crisp, clean transfer image. This works great for adding images to journal pages, cards or paintings.

LIMITATIONS
You are limited to the size of your printer feed.

SURFACE OPTIONS
This technique works best on paper but it will work on some absorbent paintings like watercolor and thin layers of oil or acrylic. Experiment with other absorbent surfaces.

ARCHIVAL QUALITY
Medium, but can be enhanced with UV-resistant spray.

NOTES
You can re-use the freezer paper after rubbing off the transfer. Just spray and print again.

After using the paper several times, we found that a skin developed that we could peel off with the transfer on it.

Materials ✳ ink-jet printer ✳ background of choice ✳ freezer or butcher paper ✳ printer paper ✳ Krylon Preserve It! spray ✳ burnisher ✳ scissors ✳ glue stick ✳ workable fixative

2 / SPRAY ON PRESERVE IT

Adhere the freezer paper, shiny side up, to the copy paper. Using the Preserve It!, spray the freezer paper. Let it dry. You can tell it is dry when the paper isn't shiny. This should only take a few minutes.

1 / TRIM FREEZER PAPER

Using the scissors, trim the freezer paper to a slightly smaller size than the copy paper. Using the glue stick, apply the glue to the dull side of the freezer paper around the edges.

3 / PRINT IMAGE

Choose an image. Using the ink-jet printer, print the image onto the freezer paper. Place the freezer paper image-side down onto the background surface. Using a burnisher, rub the image onto the background. Peel back the paper to check the transfer. Burnish more if necessary.

TROUBLESHOOTING

WHY DID MY IMAGE SMEAR?

If your transfers smears, you forgot to spray it with a workable fixative. If you want it to be a perfect transfer, consider starting over.

But if the smear looks cool to you, keep it. Stop what you're doing and let everything dry thoroughly. Spray with the workable fixative, then let that dry.

4 / SPRAY WITH WORKABLE FIXATIVE

Using the workable fixative, spray the image. Allow it to dry thoroughly before embellishing.

TRANSFER INK

If you want a soft romantic look for your transfer, use an ink-jet printout on regular printer paper, a cotton ball and transfer ink, which is slightly scented. You will get a better transfer if you use a high-contrast image.

Different papers will take the image differently. Textured surfaces make it very difficult to get a good transfer.

LIMITATIONS
This technique works with absorbent papers only.

If there isn't enough contrast in the image to be transferred, you will get a fuzzy or flat image with no highlights or shadows.

SURFACE OPTIONS
This technique only works on papers.

ARCHIVAL QUALITY
Low, but a UV-resistant spray can help improve the quality.

NOTES
This technique has a perfume odor, so it is not recommended for people with sensitivity to perfume.

Be sure to do this technique in a well-ventilated area.

MEMORY | *Transfer ink transfers, tea bags, papers and textured stamps*
ARTWORK BY DARLENE OLIVIA McELROY

Materials ✳ ink-jet printer ✳ transfer ink ✳ background paper ✳ cotton ball ✳ tape ✳ copy paper

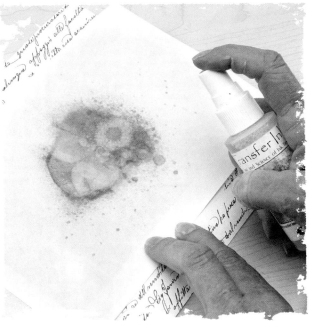

1 / PLACE IMAGE ON BACKGROUND

Choose an image. Using the ink-jet printer, print the image onto the piece of copy paper. Lay the ink-jet image facedown on the background. Using the tape, secure the image to the background paper.

2 / SPRAY ON TRANSFER INK

Using the transfer ink, spray the back of the image. You will see the image appear through the paper.

3 / BLOT IMAGE

Using the cotton ball, blot the back of the image. It is important that you do not rub the image because the paper will break up.

4 / CHECK TRANSFER

Lift the edge of the paper to check the transfer. Repeat steps 2 and 3 as needed. When you are satisfied with the transfer, let the image dry thoroughly before embellishing.

★ TROUBLESHOOTING ★

THE IMAGE WON'T TRANSFER. WHY NOT?

It's possible that you haven't used enough of the transfer ink, or you let it dry out before blotting it.

To fix this, repeat steps 2 and 3 until you get the transfer you want.

THE PAPER IS BREAKING UP! CAN I SAVE THIS TRANSFER?

Unfortunately, no. You have probably been rubbing the paper too hard, causing it to weaken and break up. Start again with the image on a new piece of paper and use a lighter touch.

WINTERGREEN OIL

Wintergreen oil, obtained from the creeping wintergreen or teaberry plant, is a simple but very aromatic transfer technique. It's important to remember the image will be flipped so adjust for that when you make your copy.

LIMITATIONS

The odor can linger for weeks and is not recommended for people sensitive to odors.

SURFACE OPTIONS

This technique works best on paper but transfers can be made onto painted surfaces with some degree of difficulty.

ARCHIVAL QUALITY

Low to medium.

NOTES

If you want to avoid the mess from using a magazine, make a toner-based copy of it.

Use the wintergreen oil in a well-ventilated area.

ODE TO A BUTTERFLY | *Wintergreen oil transfers, gel direct transfers, stamps and found objects*
ARTWORK BY DARLENE OLIVIA McELROY

Materials ✳ toner-based or magazine image ✳ background paper ✳ wintergreen oil ✳ burnisher ✳ cotton balls ✳ tape ✳ scissors

1 / PREPARE IMAGE

Choose a toner-based or magazine image. Using the scissors, cut out the desired image. Using the tape, secure the image facedown onto the background.

2 / APPLY WINTERGREEN OIL

Soak the cotton ball with the wintergreen oil.

3 / IMAGE WILL SHOW THROUGH

Apply the wintergreen oil to the back of the image; blotting works well. The paper will become translucent, and you will be able to see the image clearly from the back.

4 / **BURNISH IMAGE**

Using the burnisher, rub the image firmly, making sure to cover the entire area.

5 / **CHECK TRANSFER**

Lift the corner of the image to check the transfer. Be sure not to move the image. Continue burnishing until the transfer is complete.

TROUBLESHOOTING

WHY IS THE TRANSFER SO MUDDY?

When the ink from the image runs together, you have used too much wintergreen oil. It's not possible to save the transfer once this has happened, unless you like the messier look.

If you want a clearer transfer, start over from step 1. It is better to add the wintergreen oil slowly, so start with less and add more as needed.

EVERYTHING ELSE

Some of the easiest and most versatile techniques are in this section. We played and experimented extensively and came up with some new ways for old tricks.

You'll learn how to turn a rusty object into a cool natural-fabric transfer with *Rusting* (page 91) and *Gelatin Prints* (page 82) will bring out the kid in you. You'll get to play in the sun for *Solar Silkscreen* (page 93). *Transparency with Water* (page 99) is one of our favorite techniques, and you can use it on journal pages, books, paintings—just about anything.

The diverse materials and tools in this chapter vary as much as the techniques themselves and can produce one-of-a-kind images. We bet you can come up with some new methods for old tricks yourself.

EXTRAVORGANZA

This paper-backed fabric is very transparent and airy. Though the package says it only works with ink-jet printers, we've made it work with a laser printer.

A TRIO OF UNCLES | ExtravOrganza transfer, Lazertran transfer, papers and dimensional objects
ARTWORK BY DARLENE OLIVIA McELROY

LIMITATIONS
You are limited to the size of the ExtravOrganza sheet, which is 8½" × 11" (22cm × 28cm).

SURFACE OPTIONS
ExtravOrganza can be glued to paper, fabric, paintings, watercolors, etchings, Plexiglas and glass.

ARCHIVAL QUALITY
Medium, but enhanced with a UV-resistant gel or spray coating.

NOTES
Because ExtravOrganza is so airy, be sure to use images with more contrast and more saturation.

If you can't find ExtravOrganza or don't want to buy it, you can make your own using butcher paper and organza. See *Homemade Ink-Jet Fabric* (page 38) for instructions. It should be noted, however, that ExtravOrganza runs through printers with fewer paper jams than the homemade variety.

Materials ✳ image ✳ ExtravOrganza ✳ printer ✳ background surface ✳ polymer medium (gloss) ✳ workable fixative ✳ paintbrush

2 / SPRAY WITH FIXATIVE

Peel the fabric from the backing. Using the workable fixative, spray the ExtravOrganza image.

1 / PREPARE IMAGE

Select an image. Print it onto the rough side of the ExtravOrganza. Let the image dry for 15 minutes.

3 / APPLY POLYMER MEDIUM

Using the paintbrush, apply a layer of the polymer medium to the background surface.

★ TROUBLESHOOTING ★

WHY IS THE IMAGE SMEARING?

You probably forgot to spray it with the workable fixative. If you want a perfect transfer, you'll have to start over. Take care that you spray the image with the workable fixative, and let it dry completely.

If you think a little mess adds some character, but don't want to go too far, follow this advice: Paint over the parts you don't mind smearing. When you're satisfied with the look, let the artwork dry completely. Spray it with the workable fixative, and let it dry completely. Once dry, continue embellishing!

4 / ADHERE IMAGE TO BACKGROUND

Lay the transfer image onto the background surface. Using the paintbrush, smooth the image onto the background to adhere it and to eliminate bubbles.

GELATIN PRINT

This is like a trip back to your childhood when you could play with your food. For printmakers this is a fun way to do a mono-print with acrylic paints.

LIMITATIONS

You must use a somewhat malleable material to print on such surfaces as paper or fabric.

SURFACE OPTIONS

You can print on paper, fabric and wood. Try printing on printed fabrics or found papers.

ARCHIVAL QUALITY

Medium to high.

NOTES

There are many design options for this technique. You can use stencils for a design, or use a brayer with rubber bands around it to create texture. You can use a knife to carve textures into the gelatin, or do multiple layers or pull a "ghost" print. A ghost is when you take another image from your painted surface without adding additional paint to it.

The gelatin can be wiped clean and kept in the fridge for up to a week. Don't let the paint dry on the surface, or you will lose the moisture-holding ability of the gelatin.

If some of the gelatin sticks to your print, just let it dry, and it will disappear.

Do not dump the gelatin down the sink drain. Dispose of it in the trash.

UNDER THE SEA | *Gelatin print on paper*
ARTWORK BY SANDRA DURAN WILSON

Materials ✳ paper ✳ water-based paints, fluid acrylics or tempera ✳ glass baking pan ✳ unflavored gelatin ✳ mixing bowl ✳ measuring cups and spoons ✳ kettle for boiling water ✳ board or platter ✳ disposable plate ✳ water ✳ brayer ✳ knife ✳ brushes ✳ objects for impressions ✳ scrap of paper

1 / MIX GELATIN

Mix the gelatin in a ratio of 2 tablespoons gelatin powder per 1 cup of water. Mix the gelatin with a 1/2 cup of water at room temperature. Using the spoon, stir the mixture carefully to remove any lumps. Boil the other half of the water. Using the spoon, stir the boiling water into the gelatin mixture. Once it is mixed, pour the gelatin into the baking dish.

3 / RELEASE GELATIN

Put the gelatin in the refrigerator, and let it firm completely (this could take overnight). When it is firm, let the gelatin rest at room temperature for about 20 minutes. Run a knife along the edges of the gelatin. Hold the pan in warm water to help release the gelatin from the sides of the dish. Place a hard work surface over the top of the dish, and flip it. Lift the container up to release the gelatin. This might take some wiggling.

2 / REMOVE BUBBLES

Using a scrap of paper, drag it along the surface to remove any air bubbles.

★ TROUBLESHOOTING ★

HOW MUCH GELATIN SHOULD I MAKE?

To determine the amount of gelatin you need to make, pour water into the glass baking pan until it is 1" (3cm) deep. Pour the water into a measuring cup to see how many cups there are. Next, measure out 2 tablespoons of gelatin for every 1 cup of water. For example, if the pan holds 4 cups of water, you will need 8 tablespoons of gelatin. One package of gelatin is about 1 tablespoon.

WHY IS THE GELATIN FALLING APART?

If the gelatin starts to break up, this means you don't have the right ratio of ingredients. Often you can put it in the refrigerator longer to firm it up. If this doesn't help, make a new batch.

4 / DECORATE GELATIN

Using the disposable plate as a palette, put out and mix the water-based paints of your choice (fluid acrylics work well). Decorate the gelatin by using the brayer or the paintbrush to apply paint to the surface of the gelatin.

6 / OPTIONAL STEP: RE-USE GELATIN

When you are finished with the gelatin, you can carve into the gelatin to show more pattern. Apply more paint if needed. Repeat step 5 to create a new print.

84

5 / TRANSFER IMAGE

Take your background surface and press it on the top of the painted gelatin.

★ TROUBLESHOOTING ★

WHAT CAN I DO TO ADD TEXTURE TO THIS TRANSFER?

There are lots of fun ways to add texture to a gelatin print. If you desire, lay down objects such as leaves, strings or stamp patterns into the paint. Or even paint on bubble wrap to give the piece texture.

You can lay paper shapes onto the gelatin to create areas that will have no paint when printed. Flip those paper pieces to use them again (see above photo).

Sandra's favorite way to add texture: Paint the gelatin surface however you like. Then put rubber bands on a brayer and roll it through the paint. You'll be surprised with the pattern every time!

JACQUARD COTTON

Jacquard Cotton is an easy and fast way to print on fabric. If you have a new or temperamental printer then use the store-bought products we used here. The cotton will give you a texture similar to canvas. You can also print several images, on one sheet and cut them out to use in different projects.

LIMITATIONS
You are limited to the 8.5" × 11" (22cm × 28cm) size of Jacquard Cotton for Ink-Jet Printing.

SURFACE OPTIONS
You can adhere Jacquard Cotton to almost anything.

ARCHIVAL QUALITY
Low, but improves with a UV-resistant spray or varnish.

NOTES
If you are worried about paper jams in your printer, go with this product.

You can also use the cotton for sewing things together or using brads instead of glues or gels. The cotton can go over some textured surfaces. You can also cut it up and sew it or apply it over sculptural objects.

TIME | *Ink-jet cotton transfer, ink-jet gampi transfer, papers and embellishments*
ARTWORK BY SANDRA DURAN WILSON

Materials ✳ ink-jet printer ✳ Jacquard Cotton for Ink-Jet Printing background surface ✳ workable fixative ✳ scissors (optional) ✳ paintbrush ✳ polymer medium (gloss)

1 / PREPARE IMAGE

Select an image. Using the ink-jet printer, print it onto the rough side of the Jacquard Cotton for Ink-jet Printing sheet. Let the image dry for 15 minutes. Using the workable fixative, spray the image.

2 / REMOVE IMAGE FROM BACKING

Let the image dry thoroughly. Peel the fabric from the paper backing.

3 / CUT OUT IMAGE

If desired, use the scissors to cut out selected shapes or design elements.

4 / APPLY POLYMER MEDIUM TO BACKGROUND

Using the paintbrush, apply the polymer medium to the background surface.

5 / ADHERE IMAGE TO BACKGROUND

Lay the transfer onto the background surface. Using the paintbrush, smooth and brush down the edges.

★ TROUBLESHOOTING ★

I SPRAYED THE IMAGE WITH THE WORKABLE FIXATIVE AND IT STILL SMEARED. WHAT SHOULD I DO?

If your image starts to smear, stop and spray with workable fixative. Allow it to dry thoroughly. You may want to put on a few coats of workable fixative; it may also help to spray both sides of the cotton.

REVERSE MONOPRINT

With this technique, you get two prints for the price of one: both the line drawing and a negative image. You can make prints from your own drawings or use a high-contrast image or photograph to create a reverse monoprint.

CARMEN DUET | *Reverse monoprint transfer and watercolor on heavy print paper*

ARTWORK BY SANDRA DURAN WILSON

LIMITATIONS
You can only use oil paints or specialty water-based printing inks.

SURFACE OPTIONS
This technique works on paper and fabric.

ARCHIVAL QUALITY
High.

NOTES
It is fun to experiment with different papers, patterned papers and printmaking and found papers.

The prints can be enhanced with markers, paints, collage, etc.

For an easy cleanup, use baby oil to remove the paint from the tools and surfaces. Then, wash the items with soap and water and let them dry thoroughly.

Materials ✳ line drawing of image ✳ background surface ✳ piece of Plexiglas ✳ oil paint ✳ pencil ✳ brayer ✳ palette knife ✳ tape ✳ linseed oil ✳ barren ✳ ruler ✳ two wooden blocks of equal height ✳ gloves ✳ wax paper or palette

1 / PREPARE IMAGE

Choose an image and make a line drawing using your favorite method.

2 / MIX PAINTS

On a hard surface covered with wax paper or a palette, put out the oil paints of your choosing. Using the palette knife and wearing gloves, mix the colors with a small amount of linseed oil to aid the mixing, until you reach the desired color. Approximately 1 or 2 drops of linseed oil to a pea-size amount of oil paint should work.

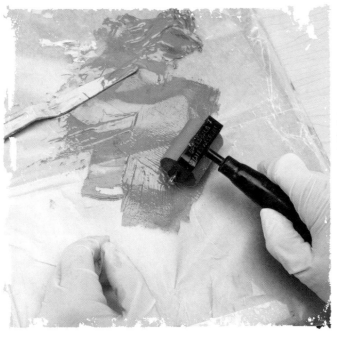

3 / LOAD BRAYER

Using the palette knife, spread the paint over the wax paper or palette. Using the brayer, roll it back and forth in the paint until it is loaded with paint.

★ TROUBLESHOOTING ★

THE PAINT DOESN'T SEEM RIGHT. HOW CAN I FIX IT?

When mixing the paint in step 2, you want the consistency of the paint to be buttery, not sticky or slippery.

If the paint is slippery, you've added too much of the linseed oil. To fix this, add more paint a little at a time, until the mixture reaches a buttery consistency. Be sure to mix well after each addition of paint.

If the paint mixture is too sticky, then you've added too much paint. Add more linseed oil, a bit at a time, and mix well until you reach the right consistency.

4 / APPLY PAINT TO PLEXIGLAS

Using the brayer, coat the piece of Plexiglas evenly with the paint. Paint an area the size of the selected image.

TIP
To ensure even coverage when painting the Plexiglas, you can hold it up to a light source to check for missing spots prior to making your monoprint.

5 / SECURE PRINTMAKING PAPER

Carefully lay the printmaking paper over the painted area. Using the tape, secure the paper to the Plexiglas, being careful not to touch the surface.

6 / TRACE IMAGE

Lay the paper with the line drawing over the printmaking paper. Using the tape, secure the image onto the printmaking paper. Using two pieces of wood and a ruler, create a bridge to keep from touching the surface. Using a pencil, trace the line image.

TIP
Using a colored pencil will allow you to see where you've already traced over the image.

8 / PREPARE SECOND IMAGE

When you are satisfied with the tracing, peel off the image. Hold up the Plexiglas to a light source to see the image you'll get in the next few steps. If desired, add marks using various tools.

7 / CHECK TRANSFER

Peel back the image carefully to check the transfer.

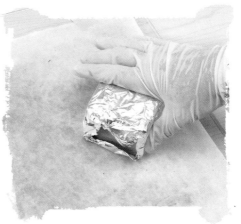

9 / RUB SECOND IMAGE

Lay the second piece of clean paper over the painted surface. Using the tape, secure the paper to the Plexiglas. Using the barren or a clean brayer, rub the paper.

★ TROUBLESHOOTING ★

WHY ARE THERE SMUDGES ON MY PRINT?

Smudges are usually a result of your hand pressing against the paper as you trace the image. If you want the cleanest lines possible, use the wood blocks and ruler in step 6.

I DECIDED TO USE A HEAVY PAPER, AND THE TRANSFER IS REALLY LIGHT. CAN I USE THIS PAPER?

You can use most papers with this technique. If you choose a heavier paper, it helps to mist the paper with water. Lighter-weight papers can usually be used dry.

10 / CHECK TRANSFER

Peel back the paper to check the transfer. Continue braying until the desired transfer is reached.

90

RUSTING

Rusting objects is an easy and fun way to get somewhat abstracted transfers. We are both scavengers, always on the lookout for items that will translate and be re-purposed into art projects. Old rusty objects work great for transferring onto fabric. This is a wonderful method for inspiring a project. Start with the rust transfer on fabric, and see where it leads you.

SOL QUEEN | *Rust transfers with fabric and dimensional embellishments*
ARTWORK BY DARLENE OLIVIA McELROY

LIMITATIONS
This technique can take a while to achieve a deep-colored transfer. You also have to keep the fabric moist with water and keep adding salt.
The color of the transfer will always be an orange-brown.

SURFACE OPTIONS
This technique works great on natural fabrics; it can work on some papers.

ARCHIVAL QUALITY
Medium, but we recommend spraying the dried fabric with a preservative and finishing the artwork with a UV-resistant varnish.

NOTES
The more orange the rust, the better this technique works.

Materials ✳ rusty object with a heavy build-up of iron oxide (will be orange) ✳ all natural fabric ✳ salt ✳ spray bottle of water ✳ trap or plastic bag ✳ paper towel

2 / WET FABRIC

Using the spray bottle with water, thoroughly wet the fabric.

1 / PREPARE RUSTY OBJECT

Protect your working surface from getting wet with a plastic tarp or bag. Place the rusted object on a few layers of paper towels. Place a layer of the natural fiber fabric over it.

3 / SALT FABRIC

Press the fabric into the rusted object. Sprinkle a generous amount of salt over the fabric. Using the spray bottle, wet the fabric again. Be sure to keep the fabric from moving over the object.

TROUBLESHOOTING

HOW CAN I ACHIEVE A REALLY STRONG TRANSFER?

Here are a few tips:

Have the wet fabric touching as much of the surface as possible. You should be able to see a strong outline of the rusty object. If there are bubbles, the fabric is not pressed against the object well.

Choose the right materials. A really rusty object will make for a better transfer to the fabric. Natural fabrics work faster and better than synthetics.

Finally, be patient. This transfer can take some time to achieve a strong image. Be sure the fabric never dries out; it must be wet to keep the transfer active. And be generous with the salt.

4 / CHECK TRANSFER

Let the fabric sit for several hours or even overnight. Continue to keep the fabric wet, and add salt as desired. When you are satisfied with the transfer, let the fabric dry. Rinse the salt off the fabric. Let the fabric dry again before adding it to any artwork.

SOLAR SILKSCREEN

COFFEE TIME | *Solar silkscreen transfer, stamping and embellishments*
ARTWORK BY DARLENE OLIVIA McELROY

Materials
✳ PhotoEZ film ✳ high-contrast black-and-white ink-jet or toner-based image ✳ copy paper or transparency ✳ background surface ✳ exposure frame (see Notes to make one) ✳ tray with water ✳ heavy body acrylic paint ✳ rigid piece of plastic, like an old credit card, or palette knife ✳ paintbrush ✳ sunlight ✳ watch or timer ✳ scissors ✳ binder clips ✳ foam plate ✳ towel

PhotoEZ film is a wonderful for creating silkscreens that can be used with acrylic paints. This method can be used like you would a stamp, but it will work on curved surfaces. You can use it with paints for glass or ceramics as well.

Unlike a stencil, you don't have to worry about cutting the image out correctly.

LIMITATIONS
It is limited to the size of the PhotoEZ film.

SURFACE OPTIONS
You can use the silkscreen to print onto any surface using the appropriate paint for wood, metal, glass, etc. You can also use it to etch glass.

ARCHIVAL QUALITY
The archival quality is as good as the paint you use.

NOTES
It is preferable that the screen is in the dark before exposing it to sunlight. Work with the least amount of light possible until you get comfortable enough with the process to turn out the lights.

To create the image, use a computer program to make a high-contrast image. If you don't know how to do this, go to a print shop and ask them to help you make a high-contrast photocopy.

If you are printing on your ink-jet or laser printer at home, use an everyday copy paper (20 lb./84 brightness or less) and print on a high quality setting. You may also print the image onto a transparency (see different exposure times in step 4).

You could buy an exposure frame, or you can make one yourself, as we have done. Attach a piece of black felt to a particle board. Get a piece of Plexiglas trimmed to the same size as the particle board. Hold it all together with four or more binder clips.

1 / PREPARE IMAGE

Print the high-contrast image on either the copy paper or the transparency using the high quality setting on your printer. The image should be at least ½" (1cm) smaller than the PhotoEZ film. Place the image face up on the Plexiglas.

2 / REMOVE PHOTOEZ FILM BACKING

Using the scissors, cut the PhotoEZ film to the desired size. Peel the backing off of the PhotoEZ film.

3 / ASSEMBLE EXPOSURE FRAME

Place the film shiny-side down over the image. Place the black felt board on top. Using the clips, secure the boards together. Flip the frame over. Immediately cover the image with the towel.

TIP

Temperature doesn't affect this transfer technique, but the technique will take less time in summer months than in the winter. The sun is more intense both in the warmer months and at midday. Your location relative to the equator will also determine the intensity of the sun.

94

4 / EXPOSE FILM

Take the screen outside. Remove the towel. Expose the film to the sunlight for 1 minute +/-10 seconds for a transparency and 5 minutes +/-1 minute for paper.

5 / SOAK FILM

Cover the exposure frame with the towel and bring back inside. Open the frame and remove the film. Immediately place the film shiny-side up into the tray of water. Let the film soak for approximately 15 minutes.

7 / REMOVE EMULSION

Using the foam plate for support, gently brush the film with a soft paintbrush and some running water to remove the excess emulsion coating.

8 / HARDEN FILM AND PAINT IMAGE

Place the film on the Plexiglas and let it dry in the sun to harden it. This is a very important step. If the film is not hardened, the silkscreen will be ruined.

Tape the image onto the background surface. Using the rigid piece of plastic (such as an old credit card) or a palette knife, gently spread over and push the heavy body acrylic paint into the film.

9 / REVEAL IMAGE

Peel the film from the background. Wash the transfer immediately for re-use.

★ TROUBLESHOOTING ★

WHY WON'T THE PAINT GO THROUGH THE SILKSCREEN?

A lot of what you do to the screen before it's painted will determine the quality of the print.

While preparing the film and the image, do not expose the film to direct lighting. Work in a low-lighted area (or no lights once you're comfortable with the process). If you overexpose the film, it cooks the emulsion on so the paint can't go through the screen.

Also, be sure to harden the film as directed in step 8.

WHY IS THE PAINT BLEEDING?

If the paint you chose is making a mess, it is probably too thin. We recommend using heavy body acrylics because you have more control over the paint.

STENCIL

Stencils work best when all the cutout areas of are linked. If you have bits and pieces of small parts you are using to mask out areas, spray them lightly with spray glue or use a glue stick before putting them down.

It is easier to paint using either spray paint or a stencil brush. If you lift a corner of the stencil, you can get some interesting under spray.

Remember to let the paint dry slightly before you lift the stencil.

KAHLO | *Stencil transfer, stamping and dimensional embellishments*
ARTWORK BY DARLENE OLIVIA McELROY

LIMITATIONS
Thick plastics are harder to cut and will take more time. Depending on the image, it can also be difficult to determine which areas should be cut out.

SURFACE OPTIONS
This technique works on any surface you can paint on.

ARCHIVAL QUALITY
High.

NOTES
Once you have created the high-contrast image you can make different sizes using either a computer photo program or the ratio or size command on a photocopier.

The thinner the plastic, the easier it will be to cut. It also helps to have a very sharp blade for the craft knife.

Materials ✳ high-contrast image ✳ background surface ✳ transparent plastic sleeve ✳ craft knife ✳ cutting mat ✳ permanent marker ✳ acrylic paint ✳ stencil sponge

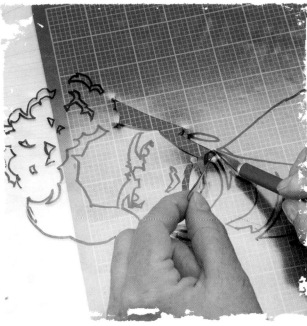

1 / PREPARE IMAGE

In a computer program, create a high-contrast image and print it. You may also do this with a copy machine by working with the contrast settings. Lay the plastic over the image. Using the permanent marker, outline the areas to be cut out (these would be the dark areas).

2 / CUT PLASTIC

Using the cutting mat and the craft knife, cut and discard the outlined areas of the plastic.

3 / PAINT STENCIL

Place the stencil on top of the background surface. Using the sponge and acrylic paint of your choice, sponge over the stencil. Gently remove the stencil. Let the paint dry completely before embellishing.

TIP

For a quick paint cover, try using an acrylic spray paint. Slightly lifting the stencil can create an interesting splatter effect for your finished art piece.

TRANSPARENCY WITH WATER

This technique works to transfer ink-jet images onto absorbent surfaces such as paper and cloth. You can use this technique to transfer to book pages that could not be run through a printer.

If you use multipurpose transparency film (for copiers, laser and ink-jet printers) you have more flexibility for all kinds of uses. This technique is fast and easy, and the result is like magic.

LIMITATIONS
You are limited to the size of the transfer film. Textured papers are harder to use.

SURFACE OPTIONS
This technique works on absorbent surfaces like paper or fabric.

ARCHIVAL QUALITY
Low to medium, but a UV-resistant spray does enhance archival quality.

NOTES
The variety of papers available today is almost endless, each one having its own look and texture. But some papers will work better than others for this technique. The more texture or less absorbent the surface is, the more difficult it will be to get a good transfer. Experiment with papers to see which ones you like best.

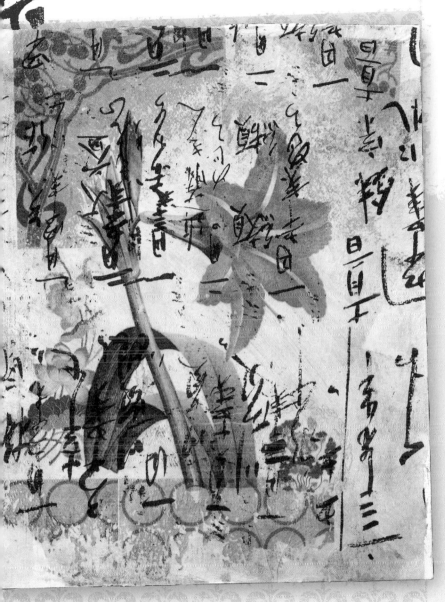

ORIENTAL LILIES | *Multiple transparency transfers on printed papers*
ARTWORK BY SANDRA DURAN WILSON

Materials ✳ ink-jet printer ✳ background surface ✳ multipurpose transparency film (for all printers) ✳ spray bottle with water ✳ brayer ✳ towel

1 / WET BACKGROUND PAPER

Lay the background paper onto the towel. Using the spray bottle with water, moisten the background paper so it is damp but not soaking wet.

2 / PLACE IMAGE

Choose an image. Using the ink-jet printer, print the image onto the transparency sheet. Lay the transparency ink-side down onto the background paper.

3 / BURNISH IMAGE

Using the brayer, burnish the image with gusto. Start from the middle and work your way out, making sure not to move the transparency.

4 / CHECK TRANSFER

Lift a corner of the transparency sheet to check how the image is transferring. If the transfer is too light, re-spray and burnish again.

★ TROUBLESHOOTING ★

HOW CAN I GET THE TECHNIQUE TO WORK ON DIFFERENT PAPERS?

The tricks to a good transfer with this technique are the wetness of your receiving paper and the amount of pressure you use with the brayer. If your surface is too wet, you get a mushy image; if the surface isn't damp enough, the image won't transfer well. Follow these tips for a great transfer.

FOR THINNER PAPERS:

For thinner papers, you can lift a corner of the transparency and spray the paper with more water, and then burnish again. You could also try flipping the paper over, wetting the opposite side, placing the image ink-side down and burnishing.

Thinner papers should be wet, but not shiny. Use paper towels to blot any shiny areas or puddles of water before laying the transparency on the paper.

FOR MOST HEAVY PAPERS:

Heavier papers such as watercolor and printmaking papers will need to hold more moisture. These papers may need to be soaked in a tray of water before using them. If it's too dry, the transfer will be grainy, as you can see in the photo on the left.

As with the thinner papers, the heavyweight paper should be wet, but not shiny. Lightly blot the paper with a paper towel to soak up any shiny areas or puddles of water before laying the transparency on the paper.

WATER SLIDE DECAL

There are different brands of water slide decals and they come in both clear or white. We use a brand from DecalPaper.com. The white will show as white on the transfer, and the clear will show the background through the white portions of the image.

This transfer is similar to the Lazertran technique, but the image won't be as crisp.

LIMITATIONS
You are limited to the size of the decal: 8½" × 11" (22cm × 28cm) size.

SURFACE OPTIONS
Works on paper, wood, glass, paintings and ceramics.

ARCHIVAL QUALITY
Low, but the quality can be enhanced by using a UV-resistant spray.

NOTES
Determine which decal, clear or white, will work best for your project. A clear decal that is printed with similar colors to the background will virtually disappear. If the colors are in sharp contrast, then only the white will disappear. If you want the colors and white portions of the image to show, choose the white decal paper.

The white decals need more workable fixative to fix the image.

ODE TO LOU | *Water slide decal transfers (both clear and white), collage, stamping and embellishments*
ARTWORK BY DARLENE OLIVIA McELROY

Materials ✻ ink-jet printer ✻ water slide decal paper ✻ background surface ✻ workable fixative ✻ polymer medium (gloss) ✻ paintbrush ✻ paper towels ✻ tray of warm water ✻ scissors

1 / PREPARE IMAGE

Choose an image. Using an ink-jet printer, print the image onto the glossy side of the clear or white decal paper. Let the image dry. Spray the photos with the workable fixative. Apply several coats of the workable fixative, allowing it to dry thoroughly between each coat.

2 / SOAK IMAGE

Using the scissors, cut out the desired image. Place the decals into the tray of warm water for about a minute or until the decal begins to slide from the paper backing.

TROUBLESHOOTING

3 / BLOT DECAL

Place the decal between a few paper towels, and gently blot the excess water.

THE DECAL DISSOLVED, AND THE COLORS ARE BLEEDING. WHAT HAPPENED?

If the decal breaks apart and the colors bleed after you put it in the water, then you didn't spray enough of the workable fixative. You can still use this decal, but it will be harder to work with.

For a clearer image, spray several coats of the fixative. Let the image dry thoroughly between each coat.

103

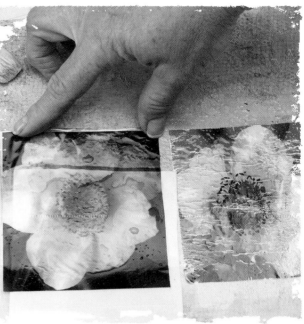

4 / APPLY POLYMER MEDIUM TO BACKGROUND

Using a paintbrush, apply a thin coat of the polymer medium to the surface where the decal will be applied.

5 / APPLY IMAGE TO BACKGROUND

Holding the top edge of the decal paper with your fingers, slide the decal paper backing out from under the top layer. This leaves the decal affixed to the background surface.

6 / SEAL IMAGE

Using the paintbrush, apply a thin coat of the polymer medium over the decal to seal it. Let the artwork dry thoroughly before embellishing.

YUPO SKIN

Yupo is a nonabsorbent polyester paper, sometimes used by watercolorists, and it's a great way to create a pull-off gel skin. You can print or draw onto the Yupo, then transfer the image. You can use these gel skins as collage elements.

FLOATING | *Watercolor Yupo transfer, oil pastel and glitter*
ARTWORK BY SANDRA DURAN WILSON

Materials ✳ Yupo paper ✳ background surface ✳ watercolor and acrylic paint ✳ oil pastels ✳ workable fixative ✳ soft gel (gloss) ✳ paintbrush ✳ palette knife ✳ brayer

LIMITATIONS

This technique does not work as well with ink-jet printers, but we did get some interesting abstract results. If you are printing onto the Yupo, the size is limited to the size that can fit in the printer feed. If you are drawing or painting, you can use the large sheets of Yupo.

SURFACE OPTIONS

Yupo transfer can be adhered to paintings, paper and panel. You can roll the skins into sculptural forms.

ARCHIVAL QUALITY

The archival quality depends on the paints or inks you choose.

NOTES

There are many ways to decorate the Yupo sheet before making the skin. You can draw or paint the Yupo using acrylics, watercolors, oil pastels and so much more—experiment to find out what you like best. For a crisp transfer image, make a laser or toner copy onto the Yupo paper. Then follow steps 2 through 6 to complete the technique.

Ink-jet prints and watercolors need to be sprayed with a workable fixative.

Yupo paper can be used multiple times. If you need to store the skins, separate them with wax paper.

1 / PAINT YUPO PAPER

Using Yupo as the substrate, create a background image using watercolors, oil pastels or acrylic paints.

2 / SPRAY IMAGE WITH FIXATIVE

Allow the background to dry thoroughly. Using the workable fixative, spray the design. Allow the design to dry thoroughly, then apply a second coat of the workable fixative.

3 / APPLY SOFT GEL TO IMAGE

Allow the background to dry thoroughly. Using a palette knife, apply a thick, even coat of the soft gel.

4 / PEEL SKIN FROM YUPO

Allow the soft gel layer to dry thoroughly, which may take overnight or longer. It will be cloudy until completely dry. When the soft gel is clear, peel it from the Yupo backing.

5 / APPLY MEDIUM TO BACKGROUND

Using a paintbrush, apply a medium layer of the soft gel to the
background surface. Lay the Yupo skin on top of the soft gel.

6 / BRAYER SKIN TO BACKGROUND

Using the brayer, press the Yupo skin down. Allow it to
dry thoroughly.

TROUBLESHOOTING

AS I WAS TAKING THE SKIN OFF THE YUPO PAPER, IT RIPPED. WHAT HAPPENED?

The gel layer is probably too thin, but you might be able to fix the tear. Lay the skin back onto the Yupo sheet. Using the palette knife, spread an even layer of the soft gel over the skin. Wait until it has dried completely before trying to pull it off again.

If you created a large skin, don't pull it all off at once. Pull a section and let it breathe for a while, then pull some more.

MY DESIGN IS SMEARING. HOW CAN I FIX THAT?

Add some extra layers of workable fixative. Be sure to let each layer dry thoroughly before adding the next.

I KEEP GETTING INDENTS ON THE SKIN SURFACE. HOW CAN I AVOID THOSE?

This phenomenon is know as crazing. You can avoid this by layering 2 or 3 thinner coats of the soft gel. Let each layer dry thoroughly before adding the next.

INSPIRATIONAL PROJECTS

This section features art pieces created by combining several techniques—an exciting way to add layers of depth, contrast and mystery to your art. The approaches for these projects are typical of how we work.

Darlene is the storyteller, more representational in style. Her background as an illustrator can often be seen in her work. Darlene's favorite transfer techniques are Lazertran, blender marker, dry gel and gampi. Nicknamed Oscar, she is a spontaneous artist and loves exploring new techniques.

Sandra has a scientific, painting and printmaking background. She often uses scientific concepts in her work. Nicknamed Felix, she thinks out her artwork and loves to experiment. "What would happen if I tried this and why?" are the questions she most often asks. Her favorite transfers are Preserve It!, gum arabic and transparencies.

We hope these projects give you a starting point to combine your favorite techniques and inspire you by showing the wide range of possibilities and styles.

PARADE

BY DARLENE OLIVIA McELROY

Looking at an all-white surface is uninspiring compared to a surface that has anything on it, so I have been having fun starting with black gesso surfaces then I go back in with white gesso to create patterns and shapes. Often I stamp with bubble wrap or embossed wallpaper. Since I know I am going to work with an image transfer that has transparent areas, the images will show in the white areas and disappear in the black. This makes the piece of art somewhat atmospheric.

Often embellishments are glued to the surface before I lay down the image transfer. It allows for subtle or ghostlike images that may not be seen immediately but that viewers slowly discover.

Techniques

Lazertran With Turpentine (see page 67) / **Gel Skin** (see page 20)

Materials

Masonite board, canvas or panel ✳ **gesso, black and white** ✳ **small paper embellishments** ✳ **acrylic paint in yellow, taupe and metallic gray** ✳ **soft gel (gloss)** ✳ **oil-based varnish** ✳ **turpentine** ✳ **paintbrush** ✳ **scissors** ✳ **paint scraper** ✳ **materials for the above transfer techniques**

1 / APPLY GESSO TO BACKGROUND

Using the paintbrush, apply black gesso to the Masonite board, canvas or panel. Allow the black gesso to dry thoroughly. Using the paint scraper and paintbrush, apply the white gesso in the desired design. Allow the white gesso to dry thoroughly.

2 / ADHERE EMBELLISHMENTS

Using the cleaned paintbrush and soft gel, adhere the small paper embellishments.

3 / PREPARE LAZERTRAN IMAGE

Prepare an image using the *Lazertran With Turpentine* technique (see page 67). Slide the image onto the background as directed on page 68.

4 / SMOOTH LAZERTRAN IMAGE

Smooth out the surface of the Lazertran image as directed on page 69.

5 / APPLY OIL-BASED VARNISH AND TURPENTINE MIXTURE

Allow the piece to dry thoroughly. Using a paintbrush, apply a thin coat of a 2-to-1 mixture of the oil-based varnish and turpentine over the image. Allow it to dry thoroughly. You may have to apply the mixture more than once to make the white parts of the image transparent. Let the piece dry thoroughly.

6 / PREPARE GEL SKIN IMAGE

Prepare an image using the *Gel Skin* technique (see page 20). When you are finished rubbing the paper from the back, paint the back with the yellow acrylic paint. Using the scissors, cut into desired shapes. Using the paintbrush, adhere the gel skin to the background with the soft gel.

7 / ADD PAINT

Using the paint scraper, add the metallic gray and taupe paints. Allow the art to dry thoroughly.

TIP

After applying the oil-based varnish and turpentine mixture, a thin layer of clear gesso will allow you to go back in with acrylics and colored pens or to layer the piece with turpentine transparencies.

POETRY OF THE GARDEN

BY SANDRA DURAN WILSON

I am a concept artist. I work from an idea or a feeling. My work is usually abstract, but I love to bring in shapes and forms from many sources to create layers of meaning, mystery and history.

The crackle surface of this piece reminds me of the droughts we experience in the desert; and the lush vines and leaves remind me how abundant life can be with a little nurturing.

The fabric I chose has a crackle print to it so I am beginning with that layer. I add shapes and forms that I see in my garden and print these with my ink-jet printer. I paint and add pages of poetry and found objects.

Techniques

Homemade Ink-Jet Fabric (see page 38)

Materials

patterned fabric ✳ **workable fixative** ✳ **palette knife** ✳ **soft gel (gloss)** ✳ **mat board** ✳ **acrylic paints of choice** ✳ **embellishments of choice** ✳ **heavy gel (matte)** ✳ **wax paper** ✳ **scissors** ✳ **materials for the above transfer technique**

1 / PREPARE HOMEMADE INK-JET FABRIC IMAGE

Prepare a background using the *Homemade Ink-Jet Fabric* technique using a patterned fabric (see page 38). Let the fabric dry for about an hour.

2 / ADHERE IMAGE TO MAT BOARD

Spray the fabric with the workable fixative. Allow it to dry thoroughly. Peel the fabric from the butcher paper. Using the palette knife and the soft gel, adhere the printed fabric to the mat board.

3 / PAINT FABRIC BACKGROUND

Using a piece of wax paper as the palette, mix the colors as desired. Using the paintbrush, paint the fabric as desired. Let the background dry thoroughly.

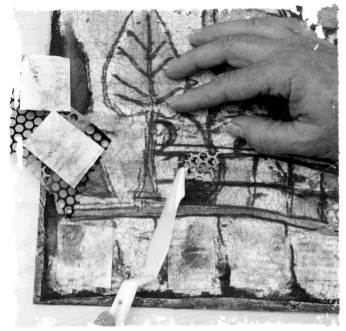

4 / ADHERE EMBELLISHMENTS

Paint any embellishments. Using the scissors, cut them into desired shapes. Using the palette knife, adhere those and other embellishments to the background using the soft gel. Let the art dry thoroughly.

5 / ADD MORE EMBELLISHMENTS

If desired, add more embellishments, including found objects. Adhere them to the background with the soft gel. When satisfied with the design, let the artwork dry. Using the palette knife, add a layer of the heavy gel (matte) to seal the surface. Allow the piece to dry thoroughly.

AUTUMN WALK

BY DARLENE OLIVIA McELROY

Being a very narrative artist, I believe each piece is a story. Normally I work in a puzzle-solving and stream-of-consciousness style.

Surrounded by texture-making tools and bits and pieces of imagery, I begin looking for the story in all elements. I want people to see something new every time they look at the art. Often you will find a main story and a secondary story in my work because that is how life really is.

In *Autumn Walk*, you have the woman walking her dog who is looking at her with adoration and making her feel special (the crown). The girl in the strip of plastic heat on the left could be someone left behind, someone that wishes she had a dog, or perhaps she had to give her dog away.

I find it best to let the viewers find their own story because mine is not always the one they see.

Techniques

Gampi/Silk Tissue (see page 58) / **Plastic Heat** (see page 45) / **Gel Skin** (see page 20)

Materials

background surface ✳ paper embellishments ✳ polymer medium ✳ soft gel (gloss) ✳ acrylic paint ✳ textured wallpaper or stamp ✳ paintbrush ✳ sponge brush ✳ scissors ✳ paper towels ✳ UV-resistant spray or varnish ✳ materials for the above transfer techniques

1 / ADHERE EMBELLISHMENTS TO BACKGROUND

Using the paintbrush, adhere the paper embellishments onto the background using the polymer medium.

2 / PREPARE GAMPI/SILK TISSUE IMAGE

Prepare your chosen image using the *Gampi/Silk Tissue* technique (see page 58). Using the paintbrush, adhere the image to the background using the polymer medium. Allow it to dry thoroughly.

3 / ADD MORE EMBELLISHMENTS

Using a paintbrush, add the embellishments and the imagery using the soft gel.

4 / PREPARE PLASTIC HEAT IMAGE

Using the paintbrush, brush over the imagery with the soft gel. Adhere any other desired embellishments using the paintbrush and soft gel. Using the paper towels, wipe off any excess soft gel. Prepare an image using the *Plastic Heat* technique (see page 45). Using the scissors, trim the image into a shape or shapes you desire. Using the paintbrush and soft gel, adhere the plastic heat image to the background.

5 / PREPARE GEL SKIN IMAGE

Prepare an image using the *Gel Skin* technique (see page 20). Using the scissors, cut into desired shapes. Using the paintbrush and soft gel, adhere the pieces to the background. Allow the artwork to dry thoroughly.

6 / APPLY STAMP

Using the sponge brush, paint the piece of textured wallpaper or a stamp with acrylic paint. Stamp the image onto the background. Let the piece dry. Finish the art with the UV-resistant spray or varnish.

MAGIC CARPET RIDE

BY SANDRA DURAN WILSON

I love experimenting with all the transfer techniques and mediums. I end up with lots of bits and pieces from my play so I will give myself a challenge to create something from all the leftovers.

This piece is created from some of my experiments with liquid polymer, ExtravOrganza, plastic heat and painted book pages.

Techniques

Liquid Polymer Skin (see page 43) / **Plastic Heat** (see page 45) / **ExtravOrganza** (see page 80)

Materials

background surface ✳ crackle paste ✳ light molding paste ✳
heavy-body acrylic paint in yellow ✳ acrylic paint in blue, red and white ✳
Golden Micaceous Iron Oxide (Golden) ✳ soft gel (gloss) ✳ palette knife ✳
paintbrush ✳ paper towels ✳ small cup ✳ scissors ✳ stencil ✳
UV-resistant spray varnish ✳ materials for the above transfer techniques

1 / APPLY CRACKLE PASTE

Using a palette knife, apply a layer of crackle paste with a thicker center and thinner around the edges. I am working on mat board, but it is best to work on a rigid surface with crackle paste.

2 / PAINT CRACKLE PASTE

Let the crackle paste dry thoroughly. It may take 24 hours for all the cracks to develop. Do not force dry. Using a paintbrush, paint the crackle paste using the yellow heavy body acrylic paint. Let the paint dry.

3 / ADD STAIN

In a small cup, mix a small amount of the Golden Micaceous Iron Oxide with water. Using the paintbrush, paint a layer of watered-down iron oxide over the crackle. Using the paper towel, wipe the iron oxide mixture from the surface. The iron oxide will stay in the cracks.

4 / PREPARE LIQUID POLYMER IMAGE

Prepare an image using the *Liquid Polymer Skin* technique (see page 43). Paint the embellishments. Using the scissors, cut the embellishments into the desired shapes. Using the paintbrush and the soft gel, adhere the embellishments and the liquid polymer image to the background. Let the artwork dry.

5 / PREPARE PLASTIC HEAT IMAGE

Using the paintbrush, paint a border around the background with the red acrylic paint. Using the soft gel, adhere more embellishments as desired. Prepare an image using the *Plastic Heat* technique (see page 45). Using the scissors, cut the image into any desired shapes. Using the paintbrush and soft gel, adhere the shapes to the background.

6 / PREPARE EXTRAVORGANZA IMAGE

Prepare an image using the ExtravOrganza technique (see page 80). Using the scissors, cut the image into the desired shapes. Using the paintbrush and soft gel, adhere the shapes to the background. Allow the piece to dry thoroughly.

7 / APPLY LIGHT MOLDING PASTE

Using the stencil and the palette knife, apply light molding paste through the stencil to the background.

8 / PAINT MOLDING PASTE

Carefully pull the stencil off. Using the paper towel, wipe up any mistakes. Allow the molding paste to dry thoroughly. If desired, paint the molding paste with blue acrylic paint mixed with white. Let the art dry. Finish with a spray varnish

TIP

If you don't want to use all of the stencil pattern, use masking tape to cover the pieces you don't want to use.

RESOURCES

Check your local art supply retailer for these or
similar supplies, or call the manufacturer directly
to find a supplier near you.

BLOCKHEADS PAPER ARTS
www.blockheadstamps.com/ink_transfer.html
Transfer Ink™

DANIEL SMITH ARTISTS MATERIALS
www.danielsmith.com
gum arabic, printmaking supplies

DECALPAPER.COM
www.decalpaper.com
water slide decals

DOVER PUBLICATIONS
www.doverpublications.com
copyright-free images

EZSCREENPRINT
www.ezscreenprint.com
PhotoEZ film

GOLDEN ARTIST COLORS
www.goldenpaints.com
paints, gels, polymer medium and Digital Ground

HARDWARE STORES
heat gun, caulk, sandpaper

INKAID
www.inkaid1.com
inkAID

JACQUARD PRODUCTS
www.jacquardproducts.com
ExtravOrganza, cotton, silk sheets

KRYLON
www.krylon.com
Crystal Clear, workable fixative, Preserve It!

LAZERTRAN
www.lazertran.com
Lazertran products

LIQUITEX
www.liquitex.com
paint, art supplies, gels and mediums

OFFICE SUPPLY STORES
*multipurpose transparency film,
plastic sleeves, t-shirt transfers*

PAPERARTS.COM
www.paperarts.com
gampi/silk tissue

PHARMACIES
wintergreen oil, cotton balls, gloves

SCULPEY
www.sculpey.com
polymer clay

YUPO WORLDWIDE
www.yupo.com
Yupo paper

INDEX

EXPLORE THE CREATIVE POSSIBILITIES WITH THESE NORTH LIGHT BOOKS

BOOK + ART
Dorothy Simpson Krause

In this in-depth look at the book itself as art, you'll be guided through a wide variety of binding techniques and structure styles, topped off with plenty of inspiration for transforming books into works of art. You'll see the form and function of a book in a new light, viewing it as a new form of creative expression.

ISBN-13: 978-1-60061-154-4
ISBN-10: 1-60061-154-0
paperback with flaps, 144 pages, Z2489

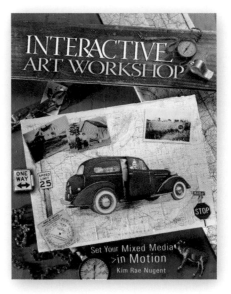

INTERACTIVE ART WORKSHOP
Kim Rae Nugent

Interactive Art Workshop guides you through 25 step-by-step projects featuring interactive elements, ranging from spinning wheels to pull tabs, flapping doors and more. Techniques for adding touch, smell and sound are also demonstrated. A gallery of inspirational art follows each tutorial.

ISBN 13: 978-1-60061-080-6
ISBN 10: 1-60061-080-3
paperback, 128 pages, Z1928

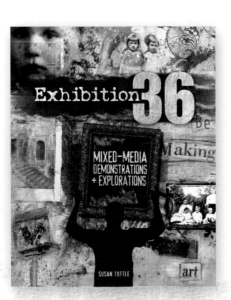

EXHIBITION 36
Susan Tuttle

Inside *Exhibition 36*, you'll enter a virtual gallery featuring the work of thirty-six mixed-media artists. Wander through the virtual exhibits and take inspiration from collage, digital art, assemblage, and altered and repurposed artwork. As a bonus, you'll find imagery contributed by the artists for you to use in your own creations.

ISBN-13: 978-1-60061-104-9
ISBN-10: 1-60061-104-4
paperback, 144 pages, Z2065